Cambridge Studies in French

MALLARMÉ'S PROSE POEMS

Cambridge Studies in French

General editor: MALCOLM BOWIE

MALLARMÉ'S PROSE POEMS

A CRITICAL STUDY

ROBERT GREER COHN

Professor of French
Stanford University

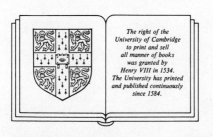

The right of the
University of Cambridge
to print and sell
all manner of books
was granted by
Henry VIII in 1534.
The University has printed
and published continuously
since 1584.

CAMBRIDGE UNIVERSITY PRESS

CAMBRIDGE

NEW YORK   NEW ROCHELLE

MELBOURNE   SYDNEY

Published by the Press Syndicate of the University of Cambridge
The Pitt Building, Trumpington Street, Cambridge CB2 1RP
32 East 57th Street, New York, NY 10022, USA
10 Stamford Road, Oakleigh, Melbourne 3166, Australia

First published 1987

Printed in Great Britain at
the University Press, Cambridge

British Library cataloguing in publication data
Cohn, Robert Greer
Mallarmé's prose poems: a critical study.
(Cambridge studies in French)
1. Mallarmé, Stéphane – Criticism and interpretation
I. Title
841′.8   PQ2344.Z

Library of Congress cataloguing in publication data
Cohn, Robert Greer.
Mallarmé's prose poems.
(Cambridge studies in French)
Bibliography.
1. Mallarmé, Stéphane, 1842–1898 – Criticism and interpretation.
2. Mallarmé, Stéphane, 1842–1898 – Prose.
3. Prose poems, French – History and criticism.
I. Title. II. Series.
PQ2344.Z5C568   1987   841′.8   87–6580

ISBN 0 521 32552 8

For Margaret

CONTENTS

NOTE

Numbers without other indication refer to
the Pléiade edition of the *Œuvres complètes*.

INTRODUCTION

Poetry and prose are an immemorial pair, endlessly quarreling and making up like a couple of Beckett characters; one tends to be tall and intense, the other rather broad and on-babbling, parallel to metaphor and metonymy (but not limited to them) as well as sexual dialectic. They are inclined to cross, like the sexes, in all sorts of ways, at times producing highly "individuated" – i.e. with strong representation of both poles – results, textually. Though I use the term "poles", as they are traditionally and relaxedly used, it should be patent from the introduction of the current coinage of "metaphor" and "metonymy" that the crossing is more accurately seen as dimensional.

In "A Poetry Prose Cross,"[1] along with some distinguished colleagues, I try to show how this seminal strand of our psychic evolution develops into the modern prose poem beginning, for convenience, with Aloysius Bertrand and his *Gaspard de la Nuit*, during the Romantic period (1842). The next big step is Baudelaire's *Spleen de Paris* (1869); its preface pays full homage to Bertrand. Mallarmé, whose major efforts in this genre run from his early twenties (1864) until his death, is another noteworthy phase; he too honors Bertrand as well as Baudelaire.

How important are these works? Not much attention has been paid to them, but, upon re-reading them after a lifetime devoted to studying Mallarmé, I find them persistently exhilarating. Mallarmé is such a rarely and rawly *authentic* writer, even in these pieces which he called self-deprecatingly – though ambiguously – "Pages oubliées" and "Anecdotes ou Poëmes." But he spoke that way about most of his writings, including the *Poésies*, which he called "exercices," "comme on essaie les becs de sa plume," and he referred to his critical volume as "Divagations." Baudelaire before him had treated his experiments in the genre very casually, particularly in the preface, where his remarks are at times jocular, even frivolous. As Henri Peyre rightly insists – in opposition to

1

those who, like Philippe Soupault, see them as high points of Baudelairean art – the texts are a very mixed bag. Sometimes the injection of anecdotal, relaxed – at times point-scoring and vindictive – prose produces flat and dull fare. But the reverse can and does happen: the challenge of making the ordinary into magic sometimes results in a dialectical progression. Understatement, in the form of conversation with Laforgue, Eliot, Pound; realism, generally with the impressionists and their literary contemporaries; science (in naturalism) – all can, in the right hands on the right days, "take off" into something refreshing, daring, superior. The *heurté* aspect of imagery alluded to in the preface and the cobblestones and wrinkled cheeks found in the texts, represent a sort of metonymy, a jumbled variety, as well as a broad and tolerant perspective of flowing charity to the Other, along this newly-emphasized horizontal of the imaginative mind, and the dirt-grooved modern metropolis, Eliot keenly observes, is in Baudelaire occasionally raised to "poetry of the first intensity."

The city,[2] in this sense, is the constant background of Mallarmé's prose poems. Moreover, given the epistemological cross of dimensions, we should not be surprised that, at the surface of these texts, as so often in Bertrand and Baudelaire – notably, the latter's masterly *Les Fenêtres* – in the imagery, there should appear windows or something like them. This, as we shall see, is almost always the case with Mallarmé. And along this challenging new way, he usually surpasses his forbears in density and intimacy.

This brings us to a trendy and touchy critical point: were Baudelaire and Mallarmé, as various Young Turks would have it, "deconstructing" poetry and Romantic subjectivism, burning what they had adored? Not really: rather, they were trying out a challenging manoeuver in an attempt to *raise* poetry and prose to a higher synthesis. It is a risky enterprise, and sometimes they fail. It does not matter, incidentally, whether you see poetry as enhancing prose or the reverse – both ways have resulted in classics as well as flops – but the patent fact is that these symbolists were artists, poets, visionaries first and last and that only some form of tiredness could make them seem to be giving up on what often seemed more precious than life to them. Mauron convincingly shows, for example,[3] that Baudelaire was ailing, ageing, crochety and miserable when he wrote some of the meaner pieces of *Spleen de Paris* (as well as *Pauvre Belgique*), but as I try to clarify in a recent essay,[4] the very texts that the deconstructionists cite to make their sceptical case demonstrate, on a closer reading, the very opposite. Rather, it is a sort of Byzantine critical fatigue, an unwillingness to renew the fertile mainstream of our tradition, that explains these easy, arriviste putsches (*cf.* the excessive fuss made over the *fragment* in our time).

In his final masterpiece, *Un Coup de Dés jamais n'abolira le Hasard*, Mallarmé, like Proust and Joyce, tries for an ultimate crossing of the two ancestral genres and says so in his brief Preface, but the last words of that, confirming our perception, are "la Poésie – unique Source." There is no real ambiguity there any more than in his "On ne peut se passer d'Eden." The work is entitled proudly "Poëme" (the better-known line quoted above is a sub-title).

Mallarmé's prose poems, in brief, are, together with the *poésies* (and, naturally, in terms of genre, complementary to them) very much on the way to his fullest artistic vision and, accordingly, though they complicate and challenge poetry, never forsake it: at their best, it is rather the contrary case. Although the scale is greatly different, *mutatis mutandis*, the situation is like that of Proust, whose vast novel is admired most of all for its poetry by many, notably Mauriac.

In the special case of *Le Démon de l'Analogie*, which I put first in my study for that reason, an enormous amount of his developing insights and obsessions have been packed into one short text, which has fascinated and puzzled readers for a century. It is indeed only by opening up its meaning along a large number of divergent lines through Mallarmé's intensely evolving and crystallizing artistic universe that we can begin to understand what it is saying.

After that, I treat the others in order as he presented them.[5] There is an early group consisting of the first six, written and published around his twenty-second year (1864), an intermediate one (1875), and a later group of six, which appeared in his forties and fifties, during the Paris years, after 1885. These are usually more complex, consonant with his difficult later manner, but none the less very readable particularly with the help of a few tips, which I endeavor to provide. They are *exquisite* difficulties, in a rich sense of that word, affording rare, subtle, sophisticated aesthetic delight, often akin to the vibrant, fluvial tone of his impressionist friends (a clear example being Monet, in the case of *Le Nénuphar blanc*).

Whatever else I have to say about these texts will be found in the individual chapters. I do not deal much with biographical facts except insofar as they shed some direct light on a given work. Some scholarly indications will be found in endnotes and appendices. But my main purpose is to comment on these prose poems in the terms which I have made familiar to those of Mallarmé's readers who have looked into my studies over many years, since I began writing on him in 1940. My assumption is that anyone interested in these pieces is likely to know the important facts about the poet's life and career; it becomes wearisome to rehearse them in book after book. Besides, the scholarly ground has been prepared in an excellent study – the only complete one on the subject – by Ursula Franklin.[6] I refer to her often and am grateful to her researches and insights. Suzanne Bernard, in her earlier, comprehensive comment on the hybrid genre, *Le Poème en prose de Baudelaire jusqu'à nos jours*, made valuable contributions as well, specifically in her chapter on Mallarmé. She was a first-rank critic, and one feels her loss keenly.

Three graduate students – Raymond Bach, Alisa Klein, Nancy Ruttenberg – deserve my appreciation in particular. We egged one another on in reading these often demanding texts together, and when they said bright things, like a greedy old magpie I helped myself, jewelled my own little nest.

1

LE DÉMON DE L'ANALOGIE

ₔ **Le Démon de l'Analogie**

Des paroles inconnues chantèrent-elles sur vos lèvres, lambeaux maudits d'une phrase absurde?

Je sortis de mon appartement avec la sensation propre d'une aile glissant sur les cordes d'un instrument, traînante et légère, que remplaça une voix prononçant les mots sur un ton descendant: "La Pénultième est morte," de façon que

La Pénultième

finit le vers et

Est morte

se détacha de la suspension fatidique plus inutilement en le vide de signification. Je fis des pas dans la rue et reconnus en le son *nul* la corde tendue de l'instrument de musique, qui était oublié et que le glorieux Souvenir certainement venait de visiter de son aile ou d'une palme et, le doigt sur l'artifice du mystère, je souris et implorai de vœux intellectuels une spéculation différente. La phrase revint, virtuelle, dégagée d'une chute antérieure de plume ou de rameau, dorénavant à travers la voix entendue, jusqu'à ce qu'enfin elle s'articula seule, vivant de sa personnalité. J'allais (ne me contentant plus d'une perception) la lisant en fin de vers, et, une fois, comme un essai, l'adaptant à mon parler; bientôt la prononçant avec un silence après "Pénultième" dans lequel je trouvais une pénible jouissance: "La Pénultième" puis la corde de l'instrument, si tendue en l'oubli sur le son *nul*, cassait sans doute et j'ajoutais en manière d'oraison: "Est morte." Je ne discontinuai pas de tenter un retour à des pensées de prédilection, alléguant, pour me calmer, que, certes, pénultième est le terme du lexique qui signifie l'avant-dernière syllabe des vocables, et son apparition, le reste mal abjuré d'un labeur de linguistique par lequel quotidiennement sanglote de s'interrompre ma noble faculté poétique: la sonorité même et l'air

5

de mensonge assumé par la hâte de la facile affirmation étaient une cause de tourment. Harcelé, je résolus de laisser les mots de triste nature errer eux-mêmes sur ma bouche, et j'allai murmurant avec l'intonation susceptible de condoléance: "La Pénultième est morte, elle est morte, bien morte, la désespérée Pénultième," croyant par là satisfaire l'inquiétude, et non sans le secret espoir de l'ensevelir en l'amplification de la psalmodie quand, effroi! – d'une magie aisément déductible et nerveuse – je sentis que j'avais, ma main réfléchie par un vitrage de boutique y faisant le geste d'une caresse qui descend sur quelque chose, la voix même (la première, qui indubitablement avait été l'unique).

Mais où s'installe l'irrécusable intervention du surnaturel, et le commencement de l'angoisse sous laquelle agonise mon esprit naguère seigneur c'est quand je vis, levant les yeux, dans la rue des antiquaires instinctivement suivie, que j'étais devant la boutique d'un luthier vendeur de vieux instruments pendus au mur, et, à terre, des palmes jaunes et les ailes enfouies en l'ombre, d'oiseaux anciens. Je m'enfuis, bizarre, personne condamnée à porter probablement le deuil de l'inexplicable Pénultième.　　　　⚜

The Demon of Analogy

Did unknown words [ever] sing on your lips, damned shreds of an absurd phrase?

I left my apartment with the particular feeling of a wing, gliding over the strings of an instrument, languid and light, which was replaced by a voice pronouncing with a descending intonation the words: "The Penultimate is dead," so that

The Penultimate

ended the line and

Is dead

detached itself from the fateful suspension more uselessly in the void of meaning. I took some steps in the street and recognized in the sound *nul* the taut string of the musical instrument which had been forgotten and which glorious Memory had certainly just touched with its wing or a palm branch and, my finger on the mystery's artifice, I smiled and implored a different speculation with intellectual wishes. The phrase, virtual, released from a previous fall of a feather or a branch came back henceforth heard through the voice, until finally it articulated itself alone, living through its own personality. I went along (no longer satisfied with a perception) reading it at the end of a line of verse, and, once, as though testing it, adapting it to my speech; soon pronouncing it with a silence after "Penultimate" in which I found a painful pleasure: "The Penultimate" then the instrument's string, so stretched in forgetfulness over the sound *nul*, probably broke and I added in the style of a prayer: "Is dead." I did not cease to attempt to return to thoughts of my predilection, alleging, to calm myself, that, surely, penultimate is the lexical term signifying the next-to-last syllable of utterances, and its appearance could be explained as the poorly renounced remains of linguistic labors on account of which my noble poetic faculty daily weeps to be broken off: the very sonority and the appearance of falsehood assumed by the haste of the facile affirmation were a cause of torment. Harried, I resolved to let the words of sad nature wander of their own accord over my lips, and I walked murmuring with an intonation suscepti- ble of expressing condolence: "The Penultimate is dead, she is dead, dead indeed, the desperate Penultimate," believing thus to satisfy my anxiety, and not without the secret hope of burying it in the chant's amplification when, horror! – by an easily deductible and nervous magic – I felt that I had, my hands being reflected by a shop window there making the gesture of a caress coming down on something, the very voice (the first, which had undoubtedly been the only one).

But the moment at which the irrefutable intervention of the supernatural sets in, and the beginning of the anguish, under which my mind, not long ago lord and master, agonizes, that was when I saw, raising my eyes, in the street of the antique dealers which I had instinctively taken, that I was in front of a lute maker's shop, a vendor of old musical instruments hung on the wall, and, on the ground, some yellow palms and ancient birds, their wings hidden in shadow. I fled, a queer person probably condemned to wear mourning for the inexplicable Penultimate.

Le Démon de l'Analogie is an early work, one of a group of prose poems Mallarmé wrote around 1864, and, accordingly, its difficul- ties are not those of his daunting later manner. Indeed, it *seems* to be straightforward, elegant and not very poetic prose. None the less it is a fascinating enigma, still needing exploration. The best commentary to date is by Ursula Franklin in her *Anatomy of Poesis: The Prose Poems of Stéphane Mallarmé.*[1] Here I will gratefully draw on her work and try to round out the investigation along the lines of my previous work on the poet.

The title was originally *La Pénultième*, referring to the unfathomable protagonist-phrase, "La Pénultième est morte," which haunts the poet's mind and around which crystallizes a proliferation of images that seem to attract each other powerfully but never come into focus. Though at the end of the piece they correspond in an eerie way with some objective reality which the narrator encounters in a sort of shock of recognition, this does not amount to understanding. That crystallizing process is the gist of the piece, its narrative development and *raison d'être*. It shows how Mallarmé's mind works, developing a poetic reality through the gravitation of words and images intertwined; as he put it in *Crise de vers*, "[le] poète cède l'initiative aux mots" (p. 366).[2]

In an interview towards the end of his life, Mallarmé claimed that he "had no separate ideas." That is of course an exaggeration, but it was probably truer of him than of anyone we can well think of. In any case, this distinct tendency gives a remarkable unity to his whole *œuvre* (as well as the final ambitious *Œuvre*), and *Le Démon de l'Analogie* is very much a part of that total picture, as we shall see. In these terms the reason for the definitive title (appearing in *Divagations* in 1897) is patent.

In her excellent study, Ursula Franklin quotes Camille Mauclair's *Princes de l'esprit*:[3]

... une faculté personnelle qu'il possédait à un degré incroyable: celle de l'analogie. Stéphane Mallarmé eut le sens des analogies développé jusqu'à stupéfier quiconque parlait avec lui ... Il concevait si nativement et avec une si grande force la plénitude indéfinie de l'univers, qu'à son esprit rien ne se présentait isolément, et que tout était système de signes cohérents et solidaires.

These things are well known to Mallarmé readers, and we need not dwell on them. Naturally, the coherence of which Mauclair speaks did not come about all at once – we are certainly aware of his numerous tentative moves, tackings, gropings, throughout his creative years – and in *Le Démon de l'Analogie* we are left "on our hunger." But with hindsight, drawing on the challenging synthesis of the *Coup de Dés* and much that leads up to it – *Igitur*, the denser *Poésies*, various jottings – we can see just how directly his musings in this instance were on the main track of his universal understanding, the "hymne ... des relations entre tout" (p. 378). We can see how his very earliest writings and obsessions are involved in this central evolution.[4]

The title seems to reflect Poe's *The Imp of the Perverse* (which Baudelaire translated as *Le Démon de la Perversité*), and there is a

Poe-like tone of detective coolness in the narration of a part-playful, blood-curdling mystery and shocking outcome. There are more important echoes of Poe which we will talk about later.

The piece opens: "Des paroles inconnues chantèrent-elles sur vos lèvres, lambeaux maudits d'une phrase absurde?" This is direct and unproblematic, on the surface. Experienced Mallarméans may be pardoned for suspecting some undertones in the *inconnues* when we think of that other elusive feminine presence in *Le Nénuphar blanc*, "l'inconnue à saluer," and we are aware of the rich undercurrent of eroticism in that masterly prose poem,[5] playing on the elements *nue* and *con* (and the Biblical *connaître*) – *nue* is a favorite ambiguity in many a poem of his ("cloud" or "naked woman"). The feminity is determined here by the gender of *paroles*, but it fits with the overall tone set by the original title, *La Pénultième*, which is a definitely feminine presence (capitalized, personalized), especially taken with the accompanying "est morte" ("la Pénultième est morte, elle est morte, bien morte, la désespérée Pénultième"). But the most important echo here is the *aile(s)* in *elles*, which goes back to some revealing juvenilia, e.g. *Sa Fosse est fermée*, in which a dead girl is evoked:

> Car, comme la mouette, aux flots qu'*elle* a rasés
> Jette un écho joyeux, une *plume* de l'*aile*
> *Elle* donna partout un doux *souvenir* d'*elle* [my italics]

The echoed *aile* will arise in the very next sentence of *Le Démon*. All this is alive already with his budding universe and the meaning of our prose poem. The girl–spirit revenant – Mallarmé's beloved dead sister Maria is certainly also involved, as she is in *Plainte d'automne* and much of his poetry altogether – is like a muse descending as a *souvenir* from her other-worldly sphere, angelically, with plumed wing, in a maternally protective and caressing mood reflected in the imagery here (as in much of the juvenilia):

> Anges à la robe d'azur
> ... De vos ailes couvrez ce joyeux sanctuaire
> > (*Cantate pour la première communion*)

Also:

> Que sous ton aile encore il aille au Dieu ...
> qu'un ange dans ses rêves
> Passe, essuyant de l'aile une larme en son œil
> > (*La Prière d'une mère*)

9

One thinks too of *Sainte*, where Cecilia the patroness of music is the maternal muse and the angel's wing on which she seems to be playing, like a harp, is an organic part of her mood. Charles Dickens was comparably sensitive to the mood: "I crept close to my mother's side ... and once more felt her beautiful hair dropping over me – like an angel's wing as I used to think" (*David Copperfield*).

There is an obvious, vibrantly ambiguous analogy between the vertical descent and a horizontal surging forth of buried Memory, an equally important theme of the piece: the puzzle is at a crossroads of cognate, mutually echoing (or specular) terms – images, poles – in what one may call a "polypolar relationship."

Elle–aile is a capital element of the polypolar "Jeu suprême," vibrating between young girl and animal in the ambiguous image of the angel.[6] The descent emerging from the past, a "glorieux souvenir," is another. The most important is the part of the *aile–elle*, which is, as in the cited juvenilia, *la plume* (*souvenir*). This word will arise fully a few lines down but is already centrally present in our next sentence:

Je sortis de mon appartement avec la sensation propre d'une aile glissant sur les cordes d'un instrument, traînante et légère, que remplaça une voix prononçant les mots sur un ton descendant: "La Pénultième est morte" de façon que

La Pénultième

finit le vers et

Est morte

se détacha de la suspension fatidique plus inutilement en le vide de signification. Je fis des pas dans la rue et reconnus en le son *nul* la corde tendue de l'instrument de musique, qui était oublié et que le glorieux Souvenir certainement venait de visiter de son aile ou d'une palme et, le doigt sur l'artifice du mystère, je souris et implorai de vœux intellectuels une spéculation différente. La phrase revint, virtuelle, dégagée d'une chute antérieure de plume ou de rameau, dorénavant à travers la voix entendue, jusqu'à ce qu'enfin elle s'articula seule, vivant de sa personnalité
...

First, let us deal with the core *plume*. It is already subtly present, as I noted, in the original title word, now before us in the text, *La Pénultième*, woven in anagrammatically.[7] It is secondarily reflected in the word *plus* – the *plus–plume* echo was important in a sheet of jottings which Bonniot published together with *Igitur* (Gallimard, 1925), and is associated with the "Jamais plus" of *The Raven* (Mallarmé thought that effect unsurpassably poetic, hinting of the bird's wing – with a negative coloration – as well as the dead beloved, no doubt).

The feather is synecdochic of the descending muse, feminine. But just as Ophélie *is* Hamlet in Mallarmé's essay on him ("sa vierge enfance objectivée"), there is an androgynous ambiguity, absolutely typical of Mallarmé, at work here. He *is* his muse, who is in him as his *anima*, as he explicitly puts it in *Crayonné au théâtre*: "mon âme ... une si exquise dame anormale" (p. 293); and in *Prose (pour des Esseintes)* where "cette sœur sensée et tendre" is linked to his inner duality, "nous fûmes deux." He incarnates his dead sister as Hamlet did Ophelia; later, in his *Tombeau d'Anatole*, his son was meant to live in himself, his Work. Then there is the androgynous siren figure in the *Coup de Dés*, who is the final apocalyptic poet and his graceful spirit, descending together.

The *plume* runs throughout the *œuvre* and is practically the protagonist of the *Coup de Dés*. We saw it in the childhood verse and the jottings (*plus je/ plu me*). It is most tellingly present in the *Ouverture ancienne d'Hérodiade*:

> L'eau morne se résigne
> Que ne visite plus la plume ni le cygne
> Inoubliable ...

This *plus–plume* echo helps explain, as we noted, why Mallarmé was so taken by the "Jamais plus" of Poe, with his visitant bird of memory as in the lost-paradisial swan image, "unforgettable."[8] Hérodiade herself is a swan-princess and an elusive, revenant spectral figure reminiscent of the dead sister in her purity, her "glorieux Souvenir." She is associated with similar figures, in Poe, maternal in essence, muse-like, as were the linked figures of dead mother and Maria,[9] as well as Mallarmé's own wife Marie: "Chaque jour je découvrais un trait noble de *plus* en elle, chaque jour mettait une *plume* de *plus* à ses *ailes* d'ange" (letter to Cazalis, January 1883; my italics).

The *plume* is a rich figure indeed, running from the "feather in the cap" of inspiration (as in *Coup de Dés*, the Hamlet-feather) – its floating airy lightness and pure whiteness go with this value – down to the pen in the hand of the artist, and, all the way down, thanks to the classic *penna–penis* ambiguity, to the phallus or penis, which has always reflected the other two images in lively and open imaginations. Hence the essential "Pénultième ... pénible jouissance" effect, clearly male.[10]

More intimately, *en abyme*, there is the *u* in the *plume* as the

11

plume was in the *elle–aile*,[11] and that *u* is the real germ of *logos spermatikos* here, precisely because of its subtle ambiguity between male, acuteness of sound, and female, womb-shape.

Pas d'autre mot qui sonne comme cruche. Grâce à cet *u* qui s'ouvre en son milieu.   (*Ponge, Cinq sapates*)

Also Thibaudet:

Exultatrice (un grand mot incurvé qui fait jaillir des gerbes d'eau).
(*La Poésie de Stéphane Mallarmé*, p. 53)

In connection with "le plumage instrumental,/Musicienne du silence" from *Sainte*, I have written elsewhere:

Here the main effect is the silent tension-and-release of musical "milk" from a maternal Muse (*musique–muse–suce–jus–écume*) or the corollary tension between rounded source (or lips) and kinetic (linear) flow. (*Toward the Poems of Mallarmé*, p. 274)

Compare the jet of milk in *Don du Poème*, the white fountain in *Soupir*, the spurt of "blanc et maléfique lait" in the *Hérodiade* fragments and a whole "white Eros" chain of analogies which we can reconstruct from scattered expressions: "Elle ... neige, hermine, plume de cygne, toutes les blancheurs" (letter to Cazalis, September 1862); "une tartine de fromage blanc, les lys ravis, la neige, la plume des cygnes, les étoiles, et toutes les blancheurs sacrées des poètes" (early version of *Réminiscence*); "les pertes nocturnes d'un poète ne devraient être que des voies lactées" (letter to Cazalis, October 1864). Referring to the generic *blanchi* which opens the *Coup de Dés*:

In sum, the *blanchi* refers to something like the birth of Love in Hesiod's *Theogony*: from the sperm-foam of Zeus floating on the waves is born Aphrodite. A pure springing of beauty, as a snowfall delights the heart of a child, it will spread through universal analogy to all the possible springings of light or whiteness or Form, such as wing, sail, *cheveux chenus*, goose feather, plume on Hamlet's bonnet, lightning flash, stars in the Milky Way, and again, thought ...   (*Toward the Poems of Mallarmé*, p. 262)

The intimate feeling is of male fusing with female in love, the *i* sound in the *u* fusing with the round female shape of the lips it goes through (as well as the *u* shape, part of the feeling).[12] It is an inner mating with what the male vicariously or secretly experiences of the female, the Omphale in Hercules, the *i–u licorne–unicorne* dialectic in *Igitur*, etc. The phenomenon of *inversion* is directly related to all of this and is basic to Mallarmé's cosmogony as well as Joyce's (in *Finnegans Wake*) – and many another, including that of Michel Tournier (*Le Roi des Aulnes*). Freud fully supports this notion in various essays: it is basic to the early formation of male and female psychology.[13]

The reader will have noticed the series of six *u*'s in rapid succession in the text quoted above: "je fis des pas dans la rue et reconnus en le son *nul* la corde tendue de l'instrument de musique . . ." That *u* haunts Mallarmé in the same way that it does in the "plumage instrumental . . . Musicienne" of *Sainte*, and helps explain the pivotal word *résume*[14] on page 3 of the *Coup de Dés*, precisely because it represents the mystery of male–female, or wave–movement, of universal rhythm: the way in which one inverts into the other – in or out of mating; the way in which the Master becomes the trough–grave–womb–boat–shipwreck and emerges, paradoxically, metamorphosed as his "ombre puérile." This is the source of the power of the word *chute*, which haunted him (along with the word *résume*: "tout ce qui se résume dans le mot *chute*") as he sighed in *Plainte d'automne*, after the death of Maria, the ghostly revenant sister in that prose poem, parallel to Ophelia for Hamlet. It has the male–female *u* and echoes the *Chute de la Maison Usher*, where a beloved sister also returns from the tomb; it was his favorite work of Poe; compare *Ulalume* and *Eulalie*.

In a study of *Igitur*,[15] this effect is found in the word *igitur* itself; the *i* to *u* shift reflects the inversion from *corne d'unicorne* to womb-like dice-horn (as well as the play between *licorne* and *unicorne*) in connection with the doffing of Hamlet's *toque*, the inversion of the madcap feather-in-his cap (*toqué*) and the pivoting of the hat-shaped Big Dipper, key image of the *Coup de Dés* and other works.

There are countless similar overtones in earlier pieces, such as the *Symphonie littéraire* where he evokes Baudelaire's inner landscape in these terms: "plumes d'ailes déchues" (p. 263). This vertical fall from Paradise is a counterpart of the historical Edenic exile in time, horizontally, the plane of Memory. It is linked with the wings dragging in the dust in *Ulalume*, which Mallarmé translated:

Elle parla dans la terreur, laissant s'abattre ses plumes jusqu'à ce que ses ailes traînassent en la poussière . . . Elle répliqua: "Ulalume! Ulalume! C'est le caveau de la morte Ulalume!"

The *elle–aile* echo here, the dead beauty, the *plume–ume* nexus, the dragging of wings in dust (final image of the prose poem), all mirror the imagery of *Le Démon*.

"The death of a beautiful woman," which Poe called his favorite theme, is closely analogous to the Edenic exile theme and the pathos of the orphan, the memory of the dead mother which obsessed both Poe and Mallarmé. The whiteness of the *plume* has to do with the powerful milk image, part of the *blancheur* chain, with an androgynous ambiguity among other complexities (high–low, etc.), including the pallor of the orphan (*Pauvre Enfant pâle*), the sacrificial Pierrot of *Mime*, and so on. The theme of musical milk – the two are closely linked in *Don du Poème* (the musical nursing mother) – from a maternal Muse (*muse–musique*) has to do with the intimate value of the *u* itself implying a male–female honeyed and milky union at whatever level. Freud has pointed out the connections between breast and phallus, and almost no one today is unaware of the complexity here. Héro-diade's memory of her nurse's milk recalls Coleridge's "milk of paradise" and similar themes in Keats (letters to his brother), Chateaubriand (*Atala*), Nietzsche (poems). But in Mallarmé, as we shall see, the androgynous aspect is much more developed and deliberate. The *plume* is very much involved in this sort of milky manna (*cf.* Hindu *soma*), "toutes les blancheurs" (*Réminiscence*) recalling the white petals drifting down from the dead mother in *Apparition*. In *Sainte* it is the feathers of the angel's wing which are music itself, figured by his wings as a harp (*cf.* "harpes imitant leurs ailes," *Symphonie littéraire*, p. 264) descending mingled with the light of evening, an emissary of sweet totality, equally in the saintly muse as it is in the suck-giving mother in *Don du Poème* who comes to feed his poem with her grace. The old-young figure of the poet in *Les Fenêtres* literally tries to mouth the beauty in the window-panes which are brimming with the milky azure:

> Et la bouche, fiévreuse et d'azur bleu vorace,
> Telle, jeune, elle alla respirer son trésor,
> Une peau virginale et de jadis! encrasse
> D'un long baiser amer les tièdes carreaux d'or.

This recalls the sucked-out grape skin ("sucé la clarté"), commu-nion with the total light-source[16] in the *Faune*, and, further, the whole theme of windows as communion, playing on the ambiguity of *glace* (who has not used ice-slivers as *sucettes*?). The *u* in *sucé* and *azur* plays in the merry-go-round of the *Jeu suprême*.

In *Le Phénomène futur* there is a strangely direct connection between sky and milk (*cf.* Milky Way): the young breasts are pointed up to the sky, "pleins d'un lait éternel." In fragments of

Hérodiade this is linked with the decapitation of the Saint, from whom a white Eros seems to spring heavenward, coalescing with the coif of the nurse ("s'en coiffe . . . en foudre," *Coup de Dés*), and other analogical imagery; "sursautant à la fois en maint épars filet/ Comme un blanc . . . et maléfique lait." This links also with the feather of Hamlet, whose forehead is "blanc comme du lait" (Banville, cited by Mallarmé in his essay; note the rhyme *Hamlet–lait*), and is similarly sacrificial, as was the "Pauvre Enfant pâle" whose head and song mounted too high (Promethean hubris) and who would be decapitated ("castrated"), the poet anticipated, as a scapegoat for society. Hamlet is *weaned* from glory, an orphaned exile: "sevré de gloire" in the same Banville poem-fragment which he cites. Weaned from the original, maternal glory, one can acquire glory through sacrifice; there is no longer maternal milk (true motherland, true life, etc.); *in extremis* one will give the "milk," *en foudre*! A man who looks at a pointed tower, for example, may easily have two subtle emotions: a longing memory of a lost breast on top (orally), a desire to give himself sexually, at bottom; all this, vaguely mixed, climbing toward the infinite like "le blanc jet d'eau" (*Soupir*), a sigh of sadness and hope.

The life–death, male–female inversion is fleshed out in other imagery: the feminine element is in the belly of the instrument of music, as it will be in *Une dentelle s'abolit*. The "corde tendue" is the tenseness of the *u* in *nul* – an acute male aspect – and it falls (*chute*, a key word of the text) into a feminine phase, "est morte," as crest becomes trough in the *Coup de Dés*, where the final apocalyptic Fall of All is symbolized by a feather falling into the original milky foam of ocean:

> Choit
>   la plume
> . . . aux écumes originelles

Note the *u* in *écumes–plume*.

The tone of the *u* varies considerably from work to work, depending, of course, on the context. In the "plumage instrumental" of *Sainte* or the literally milky *azur* of *Don du Poème* (which the baby–poem hungers for, right after the central image of the *sein*[17]; compare "le ciel comme du lait," Verlaine, *L'Echelonnement des haies*) the *u* effect is very positive, sensual. Here, in our prose poem, this is true of the obsessive, incantatory and infantile succession of *u* and the accompanying imagery of music, bellied instrument, *plumes*, etc. But there is also a sadder tone in the decline and inversion, as in *Plainte d'automne* (*chute*); the fall is sweetly elegiac but on the sombre side: metaphysical, fateful, eschatological.

The *instrument* of the text bears out the main point: a musical instrument is male – the faun's flute is a fine example – and also female in its hollow, its "womb" of art. This ambiguity of the "tool" fascinated Mallarmé: in *Conflit* he refers to "cette pelle et cette pioche, sexuels" (p. 356). The aboriginal concept of the penis–womb is a related ambiguity. Valéry was similarly fascinated and planned a major project on the instrument (nothing seems to have come of it). But part of the fascination stems from another dimension of ambiguity, corollary to the sexual: a tool, or instrument, paradoxically joins to and separates from. In this sense it is in the same boat as all metaphor, indeed all language, all mentality, all form.

The *u* is the core of the inversion–phenomenon in *instrument*. But the *strum* element could conceivably have worked on Mallarmé. The imagery of the text certainly refers to such a strumming, a brushing of the cords of an instrument.

The inversion or fall from male to female, crest to trough, proud doing to failure, has as its deepest cognate the movement from life to death. But according to the free polypolar epistemology which underlies the *Coup de Dés*, the becoming is in all directions and paradoxical. The fall is to feminine grace of the cosmic all-womb – reflected by the open or transparent window of "Une dentelle" ("filial on aurait pu naître"), or *Les Fenêtres*, where a person can be reborn; that is one clear direction. It also has as close cognate the "fall" into the past through memory (or sensed in setbacks) and similarly to be reborn, hopefully, through a baptismal reversion to the original Eden (*cf*. Meaulnes desperate in the sheepfold, from which sprang a maternal vision). Ursula Franklin accurately detected an Orphic theme here, and we know that Mallarmé was taken with it: the Great Work was to be an "explication orphique" of the world, and he respected the Orphic over the Homeric in the same sense that Nietzsche or Heidegger respected the pre-Socratic.

The communion with the dead woman – mother, sister, girlfriend – is a major strain in Mallarmé, well treated by Adile Ayda, Léon Cellier and Charles Mauron in particular. To venture into the realm of the dead as Aeneas did, for example, in search of a dead mother, is ambiguously Edenic and mortal, vertical and horizontal. The palm in our last-quoted sentence of the text is a symbol of glory (Mallarmé identified it as such to Henri Roujon in connection with

Don du Poème), and the *rameau*, in the text, which is close to it in place and meaning – palm-frond, bough – can be the other side of the same symbol: it can be the Golden Bough (*rameau d'or*, as in Fraser's classic work) which protects one against fatality. And it is also a Christian symbol of resurrection, as in Palm Sunday – Christ rode over palm-fronds during his *nostos*, his return to Jerusalem.

Palme and *plume* are related as near-anagrams or near-echoes. Thus in *Don du Poème*, the *plumes* of visitant inspiration are associated, as in *Sainte*, with angelically descending rays of light (whether in morning or evening) and hence with the palm of glory, and the poet cries "Palmes!" They are appropriate for Hérodiade (*Don du Poème* tells of his working on that "enfant d'Idumée" in her Middle Eastern setting, and fragments of *Hérodiade* refer to them). One senses too, again anagrammatically, that the *lampe*, which is the relatively feeble sign of the inner or all-too-human artificial equivalent of the divine light – the true Creation – echoes the *palme(s)*. The imbrication recalls "l'or" in "la moire" of Baudelaire (*La Chevelure*). The lamp represents an earth-bound beauty despite the humility of the main theme and indeed is itself *angélique*, a spark of the immortal fire.

Harking back to the fact that the haunting phrase is said to be a *vers* and that it is written as a run-on line with *La Pénultième* finishing a line, completed by *est morte*, in the next line, what are we to make of this configuration? Surely, as Orphic art it has to do with lyricism (the Orphic lyre invoked by Mallarmé in his essay on Banville),[18] which is to say poetic art. But why the *enjambement*? Well, that makes possible the graphic *fall*, consonant with the death.[19] We are here, already, as in the *Faune* a bit later, in the realm of literary two-dimensionality (tetrapolarity; *cf.* la "symphonique équation propre aux saisons," in *La Musique et les Lettres*), which corresponds to music's envied plenitude of harmony-and-melody and which will push Mallarmé on to fuller expression of this complexity in his *Coup de Dés*.

The *nul* can command some more attention: its presence–absence (as of a person, denied) is related to the ambiguous *u* in it, but more importantly it evokes a tension (*tendue*) stretched to the breaking point over an emptiness: hollow womb of lute (*cf.* the echo *luth–lutte*). This presence–absence, this absurdist wavering, is the substance of "Une dentelle," where the (sad) mandola is featured, together with the floating absent–present dawn window, beautifully pure and in a sense womb-shaped, hence a place of (re)birth, between its two so-feminine curtains.

This *nul* is associated in various texts with music and the place of birth, the bellied instrument of music, creativity, and window, pure "bed." In *Une dentelle* it is "nul ventre que le sien" (mandora's, window's) and in fragments of *Hérodiade* we have:

> Non! nul jour – de la belle fenêtre
> Elle n'a pas aimé, cette princesse, naître
> Et cette mandoline au ventre [space] dit
> Pourquoi que sur le drap maternel du vieux lit . . .

There almost, for the English teacher, seems to be a hint of "belly" in "belle" (with its appropriate *b* shape, as in *Les Fenêtres*, associated with swans). But in any case, the *nul* is all bound up with birth and music and emptiness or pure absence and refusal, death-urges and the like, appropriate to all we know of *Hérodiade*, which is very close in time of conception to *Le Démon*.

T. S. Eliot took up the combination of window, belly and music in *Ash Wednesday*:

> . . . a slotted window bellied like the fig's fruit
> . . . Enchanted the maytime with an antique flute

Oublié, another key word, reminds us that a central theme in *Prose* (*pour des Esseintes*) is the forgotten (in dusty Memory) art (*cf. L'Hommage à Wagner*) lost with Eden, or Edenic youth ("l'enfance adorable" of *Las de l'amer*) for the ageing poet. This is treated at length in "O quel lointain: Memory in Mallarmé," and *Toward the Poems of Mallarmé*. The "O quel lointain," voice of the sweet bird of youth, the "cygne inoubliable," now flown (in the passage quoted above from the *Ouverture ancienne d'Hérodiade*, which also incorporates the "O quel lointain"), the "cygne d'autrefois" of *Le Vierge, le vivace*, expressing the anxiety of the resurrection of that golden voice as it struggles back into the poet's consciousness (like Combray for Proust), all this is what we are faced with in the "glorieux Souvenir" of our text.[20] The *oublié* also recalls the pristine, original *matin oublié des prophètes* in *Hérodiade*, another way of looking back at Eden.

The sad mandora (sort of mandoline) of *Une dentelle s'abolit* suggests the fear of sterility, a theme which runs through *Hérodiade*, featuring the too virginal princess; for example in the quatrain we have just cited. This anxiety about birth was evoked with similar imagery in Goethe's *Wilhelm Meister*, and, later, in Alain-Fournier's *Le Grand Meaulnes*, where a lute with broken strings on a bed hints of a disappointed wedding–engagement (both for Frantz and, in a re-evocation of the image, for Meaulnes). In these terms, the *nul* is the tense place of a possible nothingness in sterility, the emptiness through which the *Pénultième* falls into *est morte*, graphically, creating a two-sided ("lipped") entity like a womb, the same as on page 2 of the *Coup de Dés*. Mallarmé clearly feared this in part out of his honest sense of not being a woman. *Don du Poème* patently sounds that note and asks the wife to feed his poor poem with her deeply natural milk (*sein . . . sybillin*). This has to do partly with his guilt over surviving his dead mother and not having mourned her at first, as we know from Régnier.[21] Indeed, Mallarmé's genius can be traced in part to his guilt and lifelong sense of propitiatory sacrifice. Not to be a woman – initially his core, his all, his self – is hard enough for the sensitive boy who must die and be reborn as a male, psychically.[22] But if she dies she occupies the place of sacrifice which typically (as in the Jesus archetype) makes up for being that deficient male. Where is his consoling *pietà*? Only in the sad self, perhaps: that wistful window. He must do and sacrifice in an exemplary way.[23]

The sorrow of the prose poem, then, flows from this irreparable loss and the sense of sterile insufficiency he almost always felt, as we know from the ample evidence of the *Correspondance*. A voice of consolation from a Muse, in this case, is sheer manna, spiritual milk. But would it come? *Sitio*. The repeated incantatory phrase is what our psyches come up with to obviate total despair: language, even short of true poetry, as here, comes to haunt us like a rosary, amulet, lifeline to cling to, Ariadne thread (*filial* in *Une dentelle*). We develop these *hantises* as a last resource. And around them, when better times come, our creations inwardly grow (like babies around a thread of DNA, cobwebs around an initial slender filament). In this sense the cobwebs in the window of the prose poem which precedes it in the collection, *Frisson d'hiver*, are a lifeline expanded, a network, syntax, armature, reflecting the *croisée* or armature of the window itself. Windows and cobwebs are central to his poeticized epistemology, as we well know from the *Correspondance* and the poetry itself. But the window becomes the *vitrine*, the shop window in which he will see himself mirrored in ghostly oblique fashion – as in *Les Fenêtres* – expressing again the narcissistic solitary mood, and the drama of virile creation. So when the phrase recurs as he sees himself reflected while "faisant le geste d'une caresse qui descend sur quelque chose," we sense an almost masturbatory equivalent of the initial descending caresse.

At bottom, the drama is of the original philogenetic being,

woman as ancestor of both sexes. The ontological drama – "to be or not to be" – is expressed by the temptation of suicide, the refusal to eat (anorexia) and the refusal to give birth, hence the rejection of the sexual relationship; all this is summed up by *Hérodiade*. The acceptance of sexuality and of the birth of self and the child, sought by the nurse, representative of woman as "linkage" (Goethe), horizontal life line, health, would be a profound resolution (although provisional like everything human) of the ontological drama, naturally. But her cousin, Hamlet, lacks these means, this "Seigneur latent qui ne peut pas devenir," precisely (horizontally) with "son solitaire drame!" (p. 300). It is general, this "antagonisme de rêve chez l'homme avec les fatalités à son existence départies par le malheur," totally ontological – "to be or not to be" – but it is also specific at the level of "womb envy," which is insufficiently appreciated by professional psychology. One must go to the deepest and most honest creators, like Mallarmé (*Don du Poème*) or Proust (the page where the little narrator clucks like a mother hen when he has laid his first literary egg), in order to see clearly into these anguishing realms.[24]

When the little phrase returns at the moment the narrator sees himself reflected "faisant le geste d'une caresse qui descend sur quelque chose," one may sense a *solitary* equivalent, almost onanistic, of the initial descending caress – almost, for the more open sense of the *pietà* in the self seems preferable; the two senses mutually overlap. When the difficulty of "being" is resolved partly by marriage and paternal procreation – such was the case of Mallarmé at this precise time – it subsists at another level as the sense of guilt that he felt as a selfish artificer *vis-à-vis* his sleeping work-worn wife in *Don du Poème* – she lies there cold from the lack of heat he should have dutifully provided. It is undoubtedly present underneath here; compare his husbandly insufficiency in the *Eventail*, dedicated to Mme Mallarmé, who has wearily to clean the mirror of domesticity, wiping away the ash his cigar scatters. And our present text is comparably domestic, located on the street near his abode ("Je sortis de mon appartement"). That guilt toward Marie is present everywhere at this period in his letters to Cazalis; she replaces his mother in terms of solicitude and eternal *duty* (see the letter of 30 January 1863: "*devoir*. Je le dois [l'épouser]"). And he speaks of the eternal sacrifice offered to his dead mother and sister added to the daily sacrifice which will be his marriage. Another prose poem written at this time, *La Pipe*, illustrates this anxiety about her and himself. In his letters to Cazalis he says that only art can satisfy his deepest love; but the price for this self-sufficiency is high, as Rimbaud certainly knew. And the *priapisme* Mallarmé spoke of in an early letter could refer to onanism – he felt that it, or sex generally, weakened him, as his whole Victorian era did. One suspects a connection between the *corde tendue* and the male instrument, i.e. its male aspect.

In the final paragraph there is the shock of seeing his images objectified and gathered together in mysterious elusive meaning. There is another obsessive procession of *u*: "luthier vendeur de vieux instruments pendus au mur." This teaches us nothing new even as it leaves him mystified. But we have, I think, "un doigt sur l'artifice du mystère."

A few points remain to be cleared up. First, we note a certain progression in the narrative as follows: he has the feeling of a descending wing sliding over the strings of an instrument, then a voice pronounces a phrase which he does not understand, cannot place, but which haunts him with, and despite, its lack of meaning, its *uncanniness* (*cf.* Freud's *Unheimlich*). Next he recognizes the syllable *nul* as being connected with the taut string of the instrument, and he begins to think that he is putting things together toward an understanding and tries hard to do so, as the narrator in Proust will do in front of the teacup. Now the voice comes back, but this time without the imagery of feather or branch; the voice seems to become independent, an objectified thing of its own, as creations at some point do. But he tries it back on himself, like a hat, adjusting it to his own voice. The imagery returns as a broken cord (he is less sure of it now; it seems rather to be a *voluntary* memory, in the Proustian sense) as he tries to master the situation, incantatorily, by repetition, and with a certain appropriate bad faith (*mensonge*) which torments his sense of honesty. Then he sees the reflected gesture which is at first a shock of recognition, outer repetition of the inner image (the original descending caress), though now it is his own hand which is involved. Finally, there is the more complete shock of seeing so many of the images come together in the shop window, like a *déjà vu*.

All of this follows a familiar pattern of creativity: from a mysterious germ of verbiage through incantatory dealings[25] with it or what is behind it, to its independent life and attempts to reassimilate it to a self (like a parent reluctant to let go) and, finally, its full objectification in strange cases when the outside world seems to act according to our predictions or forebodings or mere previous awarenesses; such, for example, was Joyce's delighted shock to see the *Finns awakening again* in World War II (with their spirited defense against the Russians). The strange death of Mallarmé by a sort of decapitation (suffocation without apparent cause) seems to follow this mysterious pattern.[26]

2

LE PHÉNOMÈNE FUTUR

The term "phenomenon," since the time of Hegel (*Phenomenology of Mind*, 1807), is a nineteenth-century phenomenon *par excellence*.[1] And there is a phenomenological freshness about Mallarmé's pure apparition here, as in his startling *Apparition* which probably, through Joyce,[2] gave us the modern notion of the poetic epiphany. But there are countless expressions of these "données immédiates de la conscience" (Bergson) such as "immédiatement, comme jaillis en l'esprit"[3] or the "nude" svelte form of the circus boy "jailli contre une proche toile" in *Réminiscence*. They represent the attempt (notably in Hegel and his successors) to overcome crustily logical dualities – of mind and body, subjective and objective, etc. – in favor of a unified, though vibrant, in-between entity, partaking of some intuitive wholeness and hence trenchantly "metaphoric" and closer to art. Terms such as (Baudelaire's) "Imagination," "tone," "*Stimmung*," "temperament," represent other moments of that creative attempt. One naturally thinks of Schelling, Brentano, Husserl, Bergson, Sartre, Merleau-Ponty, but this is just in passing, for we are not much concerned with philosophy, even that kind, here. Mallarmé was a thinker – as profoundly visionary as any – but not a philosopher, with the professional distortion or limitation that that implied to Heidegger. Valéry, Mallarmé's disciple, in his essay "Léonard et les philosophes" pointed out why a universal creative mind in the tradition of Leonardo can dispense with the philosophers, except as convenient references.

The future is not at all of the dynamic Marinetti or Apollinaire brand soon to appear, in the budding twentieth century. Mallarmé was capable of wistful hope for mankind and strove to improve it through an original myth, a sort of New Testament of beauty and lucidity, as we know, but the tone of that direction here is disenchanted. Not that he accepted the "decadent" tag some have

23

tried to foist on him (e.g. Anna Balakian, Tolstoy, Croce): he humorously rejected this ascription with

> J'ai mal à la dent
> D'être décadent   (*Vers de circonstance*)

Baudelaire, who had also briefly flirted with this temptation hovering in an unsure *Zeitgeist*, is still present in the young author trying to go the master one better. And Baudelaire was aware of this effort, as we can tell from his direct comment in *Pauvre Belgique*[4] and also, indirectly, from his worried remark about the fledgling poets who caused him "une peur bleue." In a way Mallarmé does go him one better; there is a sunny and marine sensuality in the stunning central woman that we do not have to wait for Valéry, or later Camus, to get. What is more, Mallarmé is more *deeply* – sunnily and saltily – sensual. He digs right through the childish to the milk-sucking infantile, comparable in this respect only to Rimbaud, or, more fleetingly, Keats and Hölderlin.

Here is the text, with my translation, followed by comments.

ε∾   **Le Phénomène futur**

Un ciel pâle, sur le monde qui finit de décrépitude, va peut-être partir avec les nuages: les lambeaux de la pourpre usée des couchants déteignent dans une rivière dormant à l'horizon submergé de rayons et d'eau. Les arbres s'ennuient et, sous leur feuillage blanchi (de la poussière du temps plutôt que celle des chemins), monte la maison en toile du Montreur de choses Passées: maint réverbère attend le crépuscule et ravive les visages d'une malheureuse foule, vaincue par la maladie immortelle et le péché des siècles, d'hommes près de leurs chétives complices enceintes des fruits misérables avec lesquels périra la terre. Dans le silence inquiet de tous les yeux suppliant là-bas le soleil qui, sous l'eau, s'enfonce avec le désespoir d'un cri, voici le simple boniment: "Nulle enseigne ne vous régale du spectacle intérieur, car il n'est pas maintenant un peintre capable d'en donner une ombre triste. J'apporte, vivante (et préservée à travers les ans par la science souveraine) une Femme d'autrefois. Quelque folie, originelle et naïve, une extase d'or, je ne sais quoi! par elle nommé sa chevelure, se ploie avec la grâce des étoffes autour d'un visage qu'éclaire la nudité sanglante de ses lèvres. A la place du vêtement vain, elle a un corps; et les yeux, semblables aux pierres rares, ne valent pas ce regard qui sort de sa chair heureuse: des seins levés comme s'ils étaient pleins d'un lait éternel, la pointe vers le ciel, aux jambes lisses qui gardent le sel de la mer première." Se rappelant leurs pauvres épouses, chauves, morbides et pleines d'horreur, les maris se pressent: elles aussi par curiosité, mélancoliques, veulent voir.

Quand tous auront contemplé la noble créature, vestige de quelque époque déjà maudite, les uns indifférents, car ils n'auront pas eu la force de comprendre, mais d'autres navrés et la paupière humide de larmes résignées se regarderont; tandis que les poëtes de ces temps, sentant se rallumer leurs yeux éteints, s'achemineront vers leur lampe, le cerveau ivre un instant d'une gloire confuse, hantés du Rhythme et dans l'oubli d'exister à une époque qui survit à la beauté.   ⟆

The Future Phenomenon

A pale sky, over the world which is ending by decay, will perhaps depart with the clouds: the shreds of the worn purple of sunsets are fading in a river sleeping at the horizon submerged in rays and water. The trees feel ennui and, under their foliage, blanched (from the dust of time rather than that of the roads), rises the tent of the Showman of things of the Past: many a street-lamp is waiting for the evening dusk and revives the faces of a wretched crowd, vanquished by the immortal sickness and the sin of centuries, of men beside their sickly accomplices pregnant with the miserable fruit with which the earth will perish. In the troubled silence of all the eyes imploring the sun over yonder, which plunges beneath the water with a cry's despair, here is the simple sales pitch: "No sign treats you to the show inside, for there exists no painter these days capable of rendering even a sad shadow of it. I am bringing, alive (and preserved over the years by supreme science) a Woman of yore. Some madness, original and ingenuous, an ecstasy of gold, I don't know what! called by her her hair , is draped with the grace of silk around a face illuminated by the bloody nudity of her lips. In place of vain apparel, she has a body; and her eyes, like rare stones, do not equal this look which comes from her happy flesh: from breasts raised as if they were full of an eternal milk, the nipples toward the sky, to lissom legs which retain the salt of the first sea." Remembering their wretched spouses, bald-headed, sickly, and full of horror, the husbands come forward: the wives too, out of curiosity, dejected, want to see.

When all have contemplated the noble creature, a vestige of a vague already cursed age, some of them indifferent, for they will not have the strength to understand, but others woebegone and their eyelids moist with resigned tears, will look at one another; while the poets of those times, feeling their dull eyes light up again, will make their way towards their lamp, their minds for a moment intoxicated with a dim glory, haunted by Rhythm and forgetting that they exist in an era which has outlived beauty.

The opening depicts a world fading through a pale, watery and cloudy last stage toward ultimate nothingness (as at the end of the *Coup de Dés*) with vestigial liveliness amidst the weariness in the dying sunlight, the reflective river on the horizon, the streaks of purple at dusk. "Bored" trees are white with age. Under them rises the tent of the Shower of Past Things.

Mallarmé favored this humble image of the artist as a natural aspect of his personal tentativeness and ambivalence as well as the sense of total decline or entropy, for example in *La Déclaration foraine* from the present collection, or *Le Pitre châtié* where the artist is a clown and a "mauvais Halmet." Leconte de Lisle, his friend, uses *Montreurs* (title of a poem) to indicate corrupt, commercial artists. But this "Barnum," as Baudelaire called him (see note 3), undoubtedly reflects his maker, *en abyme*. This is a time-honored device for time-warps, flashbacks and projections forward.

The *réverbères* remind one of those of the debauching, world-weary Baudelaire, prominently in *Le Crépuscule du matin*, which are directly echoed, or reverberated, in the street-lights – complete with ghostly prostitutes' essences – of Mallarmé's sonnet, *Le Tombeau de Charles Baudelaire*, commemorating the great ancestor. The original sin, "le péché des siècles,"[5] which is the active human projection of general negation, evil, Thanatos, the "immortal sickness" behind all this collapse, flows easily from Baudelaire to Mallarmé, as we can also judge from the lyric essay on the former in *La Symphonie littéraire*, where the imagery largely foretells the present waning scene. The sinking sun sums it all up, with the poignant focussing of a last desperate cry.

But look! there surges up from nowhere the miraculously renascent beauty of a naked living woman preserved from more wholesome earlier times. Science is naturally a dubious entity for an artist like Mallarmé, but, like Poe – and even his close friend Villiers who made a career out of its depradations – as well as Valéry, who overdid his homage to this limited form of knowing, Mallarmé knew its objective value; and he gives it some credit, for preserving, coldly, in a deathly, logical and technological way, almost mummifying, this otherwise extinct gorgeousness. The artists who, of course, *should* do this, in their comprehensive way including their share of the scientific spirit – or, rather, who should create afresh, *originally* – are no longer capable. That is the typical bell-tone of Mallarmé, in the essays and the *Hommage à Richard Wagner* and *Prose (pour des Esseintes)*. But he was planning to remedy this, as we know from the critical piece on Wagner and the rest.

Woman, going back to the divine Mother, is naturally central in Mallarmé's world as in the real world. This adoration also breeds, inevitably, moments of metaphysical, Promethean or Luciferian, revolt (and a sort of sour grapes) which has much to do with male creativity.[6] Modern minds are apt to see this attitude as "putting her on a pedestal" as opposed to tempered egalitarianism, equity between the sexes, and of course they are partly justified. But the other dimension – high–low, saint–prostitute, etc. – exists powerfully too and has its intermittent place in life and art. It is something both to acknowledge honestly and to live down, again and again, like all dangerously deep emotion.[7]

The sensual female godhead is clearly present in the Faun's dream of ravishing Venus, in the lost glorious mother of *Apparition*, everywhere in his poetic universe. Her hair stands, or flows, for this centrality and totality, in the sense that the arabesque, the ornament, the vertical yet whole-aspiring "metaphoric" – as opposed to "metonymic," practical, ordinary meaning – generally does for contemporary aesthetic thought. The rivery flow that is the on-going aspect of this centrality[8] is the tender *grace* here, the gentle undulation of the hair which, like a stream, tends toward (final, oceanic) wholeness in its elusive curves *around* the face. Whereas the stunning *révolté* lightning-like vertical aspect of the metaphoric (as we conceive it along with Jakobson) – parallel to the paradigmatic, the qualitative, the free-spatial, etc. cutting plungingly and soaringly across the banal, syntagmatic, quantitative, chronological, etc. – is in her *jaillissement*, her striking stature[9] (however modest in measurable size, she is like Venus emerging, "m'as-tu-vue?" or Valéry's Helen, "me voilà," phenomenal!).

All this is pure, "original," hence a wild "madness" (*folie*) and "naïve," an "ecstasy" (*ex-stasis*, out of ordinary time and space), golden as the first sunburst, now going under in the background.[10]

The hair was this for Baudelaire, notably in *La Chevelure*,[11] where he thought of it as an *étoffe* likewise, a handkerchief which one could grab and wave as one wanted with a monstrous childish glee. In a spate of poems Mallarmé compared it to a rippling flag, a cloud, tumbling roses, oriental silk, *que sais-je*. I wondered about the flag image until I saw a woman standing tall with her hair streaming out sideways in a stiff wind, lovely and funny.

The *nudité sanglante* of the lips echoes the dangerous, bloody aspect of Hérodiade and of Everywoman underneath, the red raw meat of Rimbaud's *Barbare*. In these cases one should not be distracted by compunctious reflexes from the simple beauty of the image in itself, a *real* woman in her original flesh and blood. Whence the "vanity" of clothes, in his terms. Clothes *can* adorn us, in a common move to totality, but often, for Mallarmé and the rest of us, they are *de trop*, part of a conventional over-civilized existence.

The eyes are a limpid transparent way to the Source. But so, wonderfully, is the "regard qui sort de sa chair heureuse"! Freud and Lacan had nothing to teach Mallarmé about the paradoxical co-subjectivity between mind and body at this level of understanding (metaphoric). Whence the *savants abîmes* of *Hérodiade* (*Scène*).

Note the *ar*-cluster,[12] in *rare*, *regard*, *chair*, reflecting the transparency (*cf. air*, *clair*, *art*, *clarté*, *paradis*, *Paris*, *Air France*, etc.).

The infantile milk-promising depth of those uplifted *seins* is equally wild. Far underground, to be sure, they link with the phallic; Mallarmé knew this before Freud,[13] as is evident from the whiteness-chain which we invoked earlier and which is very much involved in *Réminiscence*, in our present group. The "salt" of the legs is in this *blancheur*-chain, and the legs suggest the phallic, in the deep sense, even as they taper toward the final triumphant central and whole femininity at the X-point, like a stream coming home to sea.[14] So does the whole body-stature, as we show in our comment on *Prose* (*pour des Esseintes*). It smacks, legs and all, of the sunlit sea (and *mer–mère*, as in the *Coup de Dés*, page 5). Who cannot recall – breathes so dead a soul? – that penetrating salt on mama's skin, or other children's:

> Little boy new from the waters of birth
> With a pristine gleam and a salt to your charm
> Like the summery taste of a sunburned arm
> On a light-shadowed sidewalk a morning of earth   (anon.)

Salt is a mysterious, sacred substance in our tradition, a crystal catalyst that can even provoke birth. Rimbaud sensed it suspended in tears of memory of lost mother-love (*Mémoire*), white as the "corps des femmes" and as the milky "manna" drifting down from the dead mother in Mallarmé's previous *Apparition* (later, in Rimbaud's *Mystique*).

The rest of the poem offers no difficulties. "Rhythm" is, of course, the essence of art as it *becomes* (parallel to melody issuing from harmony in music) from the central, vibrant paradox (*fiction*) which is the core of Mallarméan epistemology.[15]

3
PLAINTE D'AUTOMNE

The voice of the preceding text was objective: this one is of a somewhat eccentric Poe-like subjectivity, which lowers its tone or class somewhat, and brings about in its first part an almost adolescent mood slightly reminiscent of Mallarmé's juvenile prose, *Les Trois cigognes*.

"Autumn" harks back to Poe's *Raven* and a rising, sweet–melancholy elegiac theme or climate present in European poetry since the late eighteenth century. It seasonally reflects the general theme of decline, of day, of civilization, of mankind. These analogous cycles are an important aspect of Mallarmé's cosmic syntax, discursively treated in *Les Dieux antiques* – "la tragédie de la nature" – and, more intimately, in many a poetic text, such as this one.

ನ್ನ   **Plainte d'automne**

Depuis que Maria m'a quitté pour aller dans une autre étoile – laquelle, Orion, Altaïr, et toi, verte Vénus? – j'ai toujours chéri la solitude. Que de longues journées j'ai passées seul avec mon chat. Par *seul*, j'entends sans un être matériel et mon chat est un compagnon mystique, un esprit. Je puis donc dire que j'ai passé de longues journées seul avec mon chat, et seul, avec un des derniers auteurs de la décadence latine; car depuis que la blanche créature n'est plus, étrangement et singulièrement j'ai aimé tout ce qui se résumait en ce mot: chute. Ainsi, dans l'année, ma saison favorite, ce sont les derniers jours alanguis de l'été, qui précèdent immédiatement l'automne et, dans la journée, l'heure où je me promène est quand le soleil se repose avant de s'évanouir, avec des rayons de cuivre jaune sur les murs gris et de cuivre rouge sur les carreaux. De même la littérature à laquelle mon esprit demande une volupté sera la poésie agonisante des derniers moments de Rome, tant, cependant, qu'elle ne respire aucunement l'approche rajeunissante des Barbares et ne bégaie point le latin enfantin des premières proses chrétiennes.

Je lisais donc un de ces chers poëmes (dont les plaques de fard ont plus de charme sur moi que l'incarnat de la jeunesse) et plongeais une main dans la fourrure du pur animal, quand un orgue de Barbarie chanta languissamment et mélancoliquement sous ma fenêtre. Il jouait dans la grande allée des peupliers dont les feuilles me paraissent mornes même au printemps, depuis que Maria a passé là avec des cierges, une dernière fois. L'instrument des tristes, oui, vraiment: le piano scintille, le violon donne aux fibres déchirées la lumière, mais l'orgue de Barbarie, dans le crépuscule du souvenir, m'a fait désespérément rêver. Maintenant qu'il murmurait un air joyeusement vulgaire et qui mit la gaîté au cœur des faubourgs, un air suranné, banal: d'où vient que sa ritournelle m'allait à l'âme et me faisait pleurer comme une ballade romantique? Je la savourai lentement et je ne lançai pas un sou par la fenêtre de peur de me déranger et de m'apercevoir que l'instrument ne chantait pas seul.   ◆

Autumn Complaint

Since Maria left me to go to another star – which one, Orion, Altaïr, and you, green Venus? – I have always cherished solitude. How many long days I have spent alone with my cat. By *alone*, I mean without a material being, and my cat is a mystic companion, a spirit. So I can say that I have spent long days alone with my cat, and alone with one of the last authors of the Latin decadence; for since the white creature is no more, strangely and oddly I have loved all that which was summed up in the word: fall [*chute*]. Thus, of the year, my favorite season is the last languid days of summer, which immediately precede autumn and, during the day, the hour when I go for a walk is when the sun rests before fading away, with beams of yellow copper on the gray walls and of red copper on the window panes. In the same way, the literature of which my spirit asks pleasure will be the agonizing poetry of Rome's last moments, so long, however, as it doesn't inhale in any way the rejuvenating approach of the Barbarians or stammer the childish Latin of the first Christian proses.

I was reading, then, one of these beloved poems (whose patches of cosmetic cast more of a spell over me than the rosiness of youth) and plunging my hand into the pure animal's fur, when a barrel organ started to sing with languorous melancholy beneath my window. It was playing in the wide avenue of poplars whose leaves seem dreary to me even in spring, ever since Maria passed by there with candles, one last time. The instrument of the sad, yes, truly: the piano sparkles, the violin gives light to the torn fibers, but the barrel organ, in the twilight of memory, made me desperately dream. Now that it was murmuring a joyfully vulgar tune which brought gaiety to the heart of the suburbs, an old-fashioned, banal tune: why is it that its refrain pierced to my soul and made me cry like a romantic ballad? I savored it slowly and I did not throw a penny from the window for fear of troubling myself and perceiving that the instrument was not singing alone.

The solitary narrator clearly mirrors his maker, who lost his thirteen-year-old sister Maria at age fifteen, "la seule personne que j'adorasse" (*Correspondance*, vol. 1, p. 35). The effect of this loss, together with that of his mother when he was five (and his girl-friend Harriet Smyth at age seventeen) have been much controverted. On the evidence of the early correspondence, where he speaks of this double (or triple) grief, I see no reason to doubt that it haunted him, and it helps to account for some of the explicit imagery and, more importantly, the motivation, of his poetic work. This is discussed in some detail under *Le Démon de l'Analogie*.[1]

The somewhat rhetorical apostrophe to the stars locates the grief at a certain neo-classical distance from us. This tradition-prolonging, imitative, "umbilical" tone is subtly present in many first-rank writers up to our time – Gide, Faulkner, T. S. Eliot spring to mind, as well as Valéry, Sartre and Camus – and particularly in France. Mallarmé indulges in it very little, only here and there, but the thread, however invisible at times,[2] is never really broken in him or in any other major figure. Roughly speaking, the more invisible, or virtual, the thread, the better the style.

The cat is not just a Baudelairean prop, though it is comparably mystic, in an affectionately humorous way. Mallarmé was especially fond of felinity (except for the rear end, which he suggested gilding), like Baudelaire, and Debussy and Colette. The strange softness goes with French velvety and steely delicacy and with the "des Esseintes" mood of Byzantine decadence involved in the late Latin writers he preferred.

The "white creature is no more": again, a certain rhetorical distance is implied in the epithet, along with the opposite move to the whiteness-chain we allude to in the previous chapter, extended here to candles, death-pallor (and white roses elsewhere). The combination of idealistic rhetoric up and death-haunted sensuality down is extremely "metaphorical," vertical, daemonic. It is the up–down paradox of the *u* which we referred to in *Le Démon de l'Analogie*, here prominent in *résumait* and in *chute*, a word which explicitly fascinates him. *Résume* was a key word on page 3 of the *Coup de Dés*, where it represented the mysterious crossing from crest to trough, light to dark, life to death, male to female, ideal to sensual, and so on. *Chute* is especially reminiscent of *La Chute de la Maison Usher*, which Mallarmé saw as Poe's high point. There too the essence was of a decadent sister–brother relationship and the death of the girl who *came back*, as in many a Mallarmé text.[3]

We note the exquisite nuances of the in-between season or time of day: not quite autumn, not quite sundown. It is particularly intimate, as Baudelaire demonstrated in some Marie Daubrun poems; T. S. Eliot did so later with his "midwinter spring is its own season," and Alain-Fournier with the wavering time of year, ages and places in *Le Grand Meaulnes*.

The sun seems to halt at the horizon, echoed later in the *Cantique de Saint-Jean*. The dying light is sumptuous, Baudelairean as one feels it to be in Mallarmé's *Les Fenêtres*:

> Voit des galères d'or, belles comme des cygnes,
> Sur un fleuve de pourpre et de parfums dormir
> En berçant l'éclair fauve et riche de leurs lignes
> Dans un grand nonchaloir chargé de souvenir!

I find no particular significance in the momentary favoring of late Latin poetry – it has no echo anywhere in his work – nor in the aversion to even later childish low Latin "proses chrétiennes," which, incidentally, indicate that there is no connection with *Prose (pour des Esseintes)*, contrary to the view of some commentators. Besides, the discovery by Carl Barbier[4] of a letter referring to that poem well in advance of Huysmans's book shows that Mallarmé could not have been thinking of *des Esseintes* when he wrote the poem.

The "charm" of decadence is in the faded colors of the Latin poems, as it will be in the "grâce des choses fanées" (*Frisson d'hiver*), and this is prolonged in the melancholy strains of the *orgue de Barbarie* wailing outside his window (whence the *Plainte* of the title: that plus the general mood). This is mingled with the purer melancholy of the memory of Marie, whose coffin, with candles, passed along the same lane of poplar trees, indelibly. This time is evening and the tone of sad memory "crepuscular," matching the dying season. The instrument seems made for the mood: it murmurs an "air joyeusement vulgaire et qui mit la gaîté au coeur des faubourgs, un air suranné, banal: d'où vient que sa ritournelle m'allait à l'âme et me faisait pleurer comme une ballade romantique?" It is clearly an essence of ambivalence, involving the union of other opposites. All this is very subtle, intimate, and contemporary to us, very bitter–corny, campy, pop art, Brecht–Weill.

The string of *a*'s in "suranné, banal, allait à l'âme . . . ballade romantique" has much to do with this dreary appeal, as in Carson McCullers's *Ballad of the Sad Café*.[5]

The length of *languissamment* and *mélancoliquement* have to do with a similar effect (*cf*. "la langoureuse Asie" in Baudelaire's *La Chevelure*): the *andante*, *legato* or *largo* of the on-droning, on-whining *populo* music.

Mallarmé wants, at last, the instrument to be uncluttered by others, to be singing on its own, in morbid delectation. The window frames this lonely tristful dreaming: its image, we noted, is central throughout these prose poems, particularly the next one.

4

FRISSON D'HIVER

Frisson d'hiver

Cette pendule de Saxe, qui retarde et sonne treize heures parmi ses fleurs et ses dieux, à qui a-t-elle été? Pense qu'elle est venue de Saxe par les longues diligences d'autrefois.

(De singulières ombres pendent aux vitres usées.)

Et ta glace de Venise, profonde comme une froide fontaine, en un rivage de guivres dédorées, qui s'y est miré? Ah! je suis sûr que plus d'une femme a baigné dans cette eau le péché de sa beauté; et peut-être verrais-je un fantôme nu si je regardais longtemps.

– Vilain, tu dis souvent de méchantes choses.

(Je vois des toiles d'araignées au haut des grandes croisées.)

Notre bahut encore est très vieux: contemple comme ce feu rougit son triste bois; les rideaux amortis ont son âge, et la tapisserie des fauteuils dénués de fard, et les anciennes gravures des murs, et toutes nos vieilleries? Est-ce qu'il ne te semble pas, même, que les bengalis et l'oiseau bleu ont déteint avec le temps?

(Ne songe pas aux toiles d'araignées qui tremblent au haut des grandes croisées.)

Tu aimes tout cela et voilà pourquoi je puis vivre auprès de toi. N'as-tu pas désiré, ma sœur au regard de jadis, qu'en un de mes poëmes apparussent ces mots "la grâce des choses fanées"? Les objets neufs te déplaisent; à toi aussi, ils font peur avec leur hardiesse criarde, et tu te sentirais le besoin de les user, ce qui est bien difficile à faire pour ceux qui ne goûtent pas l'action.

Viens, ferme ton vieil almanach allemand, que tu lis avec attention, bien qu'il ait paru il y a plus de cent ans et que les rois qu'il annonce soient tous morts, et sur l'antique tapis couché, la tête appuyée parmi tes genoux charitables dans ta robe pâlie, ô calme enfant, je te parlerai pendant des heures; il n'y a plus de champs et les rues sont vides, je te parlerai de nos meubles . . . Tu es distraite?

(Ces toiles d'araignées grelottent au haut des grandes croisées.)

35

Winter Shivers

This Dresden china clock, which loses time and strikes the thirteenth hour amidst its flowers and gods, to whom did it belong? Consider that it came from Saxony by the slow stagecoaches of olden times.

(Curious shadows are hanging on the worn window panes.)

And your Venetian mirror, profound as a cold fountain, framed by a shore of heraldic serpents which have lost their gilding, who has contemplated himself in it? Ah! I am sure that more than one woman has bathed the sin of her beauty in this water; and perhaps if I looked for a long time, I would see a naked ghost.

– You rascal, you often say wicked things.

(I see spider webs, at the top of the tall casement windows.)

Our chest is also very old: see how this fire reddens its sad wood; the faded curtains are equally old, and the tapestry of the discolored armchairs, and the ancient engravings on the walls, and all our old things? Does it not seem to you even that the Bengal birds and the blue bird have faded with time?

(Do not think about the spider webs trembling at the top of the tall casement windows.)

You love all those things, and that is why I can live by your side. Did you not desire, my sister with the look of olden times, that in one of my poems should appear these words "the grace of faded things"? New things displease you; they frighten you as they do me with their loud boldness, and you would feel the need to wear them out, which is very difficult to do for those who do not enjoy action.

Come, close your old German almanac, which you are reading attentively, although it appeared more than a hundred years ago and the kings it announces are all dead, and, stretched on the old rug, my head resting on your charitable knees in your faded dress, o calm child, I shall speak to you for hours; there are no longer any fields and the streets are empty, I shall speak to you of our furniture ... Your mind is wandering?

(Those spider webs are shivering with cold at the top of the big casement windows.)

The window is squarely in the middle of this text. It is featured four times in a sort of prose-refrain,[1] adding an element of frame symmetry.

The window, for art, is like eyes for the person: offering transparent access to the soul, reflecting the world. The whole atmosphere of a snug but anxious – inner pitted against threatening outer[2] – interiority and domesticity, in winter, passes by way of the window and intimately personal furniture, familiar in Mallarmé's poetic settings and motifs.

Winter–window–wind: these English echoes may well have worked on him. The tension of delight–anxiety, inner–outer, warm (artificial or remembered) summer versus cold winter, in a moment of impulsive release, gives off a *shiver*, as a taut musical string, plucked or bowed, emits a vibrant tone. Baudelaire's *Chant d'automne*, between ebbing estival comfort and on-coming freeze, released just such a *frisson*, as did his *Crépuscule du matin*, "plein du frisson des choses qui s'enfuient," or Mallarmé's own *Don du Poème*, evoking a shivery morning ("frémit") moment between chilly night and nascent sunlight.[3]

This prose poem combines the fundamental structure (note *croisée*, thrice), the window's, with a vibrancy that almost seems to emerge from it as if it were punished by the inspiring wind and shivered like a wave-emitting crystal. The cobwebs which tremble in the casements ("tremblent . . . grelottent") are, by their network shape, related to the symmetric window-shape itself; and they express similarly this complex static–kinetic structure-in-becoming[4] which is what tense and dense poetry of Mallarmé's "static" and crystalline (yet rushingly moving) sort is.[5]

The *glace de Venise* is a prominent variant on this, with its play on cold water ("froide fontaine") and the *glace–glace* (ice) echo, as in *Hérodiade*.[6] And in another parallel to that poem, where the heroine thaws erotically (or Erotically) at the end of the *Scène*, dubiously, the warmth of the melting effects a sort of naked nymph emanation right out of the mirror–water (the "nixe" of *Ses purs ongles*, the voluptuous nymphs of the *Faune*), whence the "fantôme nu" here and the sense of "sin."[7]

The wife understandably objects to this roving fantasy, and the poet–husband returns, partly dutifully, to a more purely spiritual evocation, which fits with the way he felt about his wife in reality, Marie, who did come from far away in Germany once. That legendary or *Märchen* far-away invests her with a lasting wistful charm which she deserved: deep down, one never forgets the mysteriousness of one's wife's little-girl or eternal psychic origins – "ma sœur au regard de jadis" – in a true marriage, where there is a durable stable base in time.[8]

Poems like the *Eventail* (*de Madame Mallarmé*) express this authentic fidelity. Mallarmé spoke of Marie in much the same way (as the "sœur au regard de jadis") in his early letters to Cazalis.

She loves her home: "Tu aimes tout cela et voilà pourquoi je puis vivre auprès de toi." She is inseparable from the spirit of the home, its furniture and enveloping lasting atmosphere (the mirror of the *Eventail*, as here) which hold up through a long hard life almost as the long-lost mother supported the baby on her solid lap. That is part of the "grâce des choses fanées," their age-old relationship, as opposed to the "objets neufs." The *fané* occurs significantly in *Don du Poème*, referring to his wife's domestic and discreetly penetrating "doigt" which does the wearing housework; she lies innocently in the bed, her feet cold from the lack of heat he should have provided, while he sits up selfishly creating.

To begin at the beginning: the *pendule de Saxe* is still visible in Mallarmé's country place at Valvins (Vulaines). It belongs to the wife's German past, with naively charming Rococo or Biedermeyer decoration. *Saxe* is repeated: does he like the *x* in it, close to the window's *croisée* in form?[9] There are numerous x's in the window-sonnet, *Ses purs ongles*.

If the clock is late and sounds an Alice-in-Wonderland perverse and improbable "treize heures," that too is alluring, irresponsible, with the elfin touch of the child-like in his wife that we noted – a sort of poetic conspiracy of children is there, as in Rimbaud's *Jeune ménage*,[10] befitting a sensitive young couple, still somewhat romantic (Mallarmé had not been married very long at the time of this piece's publication, scarcely more than a year).

The distance in space and time ("autrefois") gives some magic depth to the child–wife, mildly comparable to Maeterlinck's Mélisande from far away in vaguely Germanic "Allemonde."

The mirror has been dealt with above, as has the reply of the playfully irritated wife, and the cobwebs. They are important in connection with the whole idea of Syntax in Mallarmé and the notion of himself as a "sacred spider" (Vedic) at the near-zero core of cosmic structure.[11] But all that is merely a ghostly suggestion here.

The *bahut* figures in *Tout orgueil*;[12] its "sad wood," dully reddened by chimney-fire, has a great depth of dampened feeling springing ambivalently from dashed hopes, as in that sonnet of memory and grief. Those "rideaux amortis," similar in double tone, are prominent in *Igitur*, harking back to *The Raven* in part. All else here has that mild death of time and fadedness, even the caged birds. There is that mysterious patina in the *Ouverture ancienne d'Hérodiade*:

Frisson d'hiver

La chambre ...
A le neigeux jadis pour ancienne teinte,
Et sa tapisserie, au lustre nacré, plis
Inutiles avec les yeux ensevelis
De sybilles offrant leur ongle vieil aux Mages.

The expression "la grâce des choses fanées" occurs in the *Symphonie littéraire*, II.

The refrain has moved from an objective "Elles" (understood) through a subjective "Je" to a second person (co-subjective) "Toi." It will return to an objective "elles" in the last instance. This revolution through the three basic persons of grammar (with a final return, or "Ricorso," as Vico and Joyce call it, to the initial one) give another element to the feeling of symmetric structure, rounded or squared.

"Ceux qui ne goûtent pas l'action" is a reference to that somewhat puerile and irresponsible aspect of young dreamers mentioned earlier.

The old almanac with its dead kings adds another dimension to the legendary power (one may think of that stained-glass King, suggesting a King of playing cards, in Proust's Combray).

The head on the lap, that of a sad child needing comfort – perhaps from someone replacing a lost mother – occurs in the juvenile poem *L'Enfant prodigue*. This is a typical Verlainean mood (*Green*; *l'Espoir luit* . . .).

She is his child[13] ("calme enfant") and maternal, as is true of wives for most men; as was Mary in Robert de Boron's *Estoire du Graal*: "She is the daughter of God and also his mother."

If he speaks of her for hours, that very lengthening of time has to do with the on-going essence of such domestic calm, further expressed by the furniture, and its atmosphere in which they jointly steep. Outside is mere emptiness of the dead season, *sauve mari magno*.

"Tu es distraite?" A slight note of elusiveness, unsureness, stemming from the ever-vestigial mystery and otherness even in our wives, for poetic moments – like the questioning close of *Le Balcon* and *La Chevelure* – or just existentially true ones, at times.

5

PAUVRE ENFANT PÂLE

The poor – in a rich sense – orphan child singing for his supper (darker shades of a little Tommie Tucker) in the street, is on one side of a social barrier, the poet listening to him on another, even though ironic reversibilities are suggested in the complex movement of existential sympathy and deep understanding. Mallarmé, like Melville (*Billy Budd*) or the Russian novelists, could easily repeat Goethe's admission that he was capable of any crime; ah, but he stopped short: "There but for the grace of God" and "jusqu'au feu exclusivement" may well apply here.

The social opposition is put fleetingly in terms of inside–outside, represented half-way through the text by the closed shutters reinforced with heavy curtains; so the window, characteristic of the genre, framing it, is at least suggested, though it is not altogether clear where the poet–observer is situated: he could be in the street too. But, in essence, he is on the other side of that window from the desperate child, in his familiar domestic middle-class setting.

 క**తు** **Pauvre Enfant pâle**

Pauvre enfant pâle, pourquoi crier à tue-tête dans la rue ta chanson aigüe et insolente, qui se perd parmi les chats, seigneurs des toits? car elle ne traversera pas les volets des premiers étages, derrière lesquels tu ignores de lourds rideaux de soie incarnadine.

Cependant, tu chantes fatalement, avec l'assurance tenace d'un petit homme qui s'en va seul par la vie et, ne comptant sur personne, travaille pour soi. As-tu jamais eu un père? Tu n'as pas même une vieille qui te fasse oublier la faim en te battant, quand tu rentres sans un sou.

Mais tu travailles pour toi: debout dans les rues, couvert de vêtements déteints trop grands faits comme ceux d'un homme, une maigreur prématurée et trop grand à ton âge, tu chantes pour manger, avec acharnement, sans abaisser tes yeux méchants vers les autres enfants jouant sur le pavé.

Et ta complainte est si haute, si haute, que ta tête nue qui se lève en l'air à mesure que ta voix monte, semble vouloir partir de tes petites épaules.

Petit homme, qui sait si elle ne s'en ira pas un jour, quand, après avoir crié longtemps dans les villes, tu auras fait un crime? un crime n'est pas bien difficile à faire, va, il suffit d'avoir du courage après le désir, et tels qui ... Ta petite figure est énergique.

Pas un sou ne descend dans le panier d'osier que tient ta longue main pendue sans espoir sur ton pantalon: on te rendra mauvais et un jour tu commettras un crime.

Ta tête se dresse toujours et veut te quitter, comme si d'avance elle savait, pendant que tu chantes d'un air qui devient menaçant.

Elle te dira adieu quand tu paieras pour moi, pour ceux qui valent moins que moi. Tu vins probablement au monde vers cela et tu jeûnes dès maintenant, nous te verrons dans les journaux.

Oh! pauvre petite tête!

Poor Pale Child

Poor pale child, why do you scream out at the top of your lungs in the street your shrill and insolent song, which fades out among the cats, the lords of the roofs? for it will not penetrate the second-storey shutters, behind which you do not imagine the heavy curtains of rosy silk.

Yet you sing fatally, with the tenacious assurance of a little man who goes through life alone and, counting on no one, works for himself. Have you ever had a father? You do not even have an old woman to make you forget your hunger by beating you, when you come home without a penny.

But you work for yourself: standing in the streets, covered with washed-out clothes made like those of a grown man, prematurely thin and too tall for your age, you sing in order to eat, relentlessly, without lowering your malicious eyes toward the other children playing on the pavement.

And your plaintive ballad is so high, so high, that your bare head, rising in the air as your voice rises, seems to want to take off from your little shoulders.

Little man, who knows whether it is not going to come off one day, when after having screamed for a long time in the cities, you have committed a crime? a crime is not very difficult to commit, come on, it is enough to have courage after the desire, and some who . . . Your little face is energetic.

Not a penny falls into the wicker basket which your long hand, hanging without hope over your trousers, is holding: they will make you bad and one day you will commit a crime.

Your head is still erect and wants to leave you, as if it knew in advance, while you are singing in a way that becomes threatening.

It will say good-bye to you when you pay for me, for those who are worth less than I. You probably came into the world for that and you are fasting from now on, we will see you in the papers.

Oh! poor little head!

The pallor of the child is linked distantly, through the *blancheur*-chain spoken of elsewhere, to that of the wife-killing Pierrot in *Mime* and the white flash – milk-like secretion – emerging from Saint Jean upon his decapitation, and, further, to the half-orphaned and suffering Hamlet, "weaned from glory" (Banville, quoted by Mallarmé in his essay, *Hamlet*) with his forehead "blanc comme du lait," the "blanc . . . flanc enfant" of *A la nue* (*cf.* Anatole), and so on.[1]

The phallic projection of the head, like that of the Hamlet-figure in the *Coup de Dés* (pages 7 and 8) is a Promethean motif, hubris, repeating mankind's daemonic striving (*eritis sicut dii*) since the Fall, inviting lightning-like retribution ("en foudre," *Coup de Dés*, page 7; note the reciprocity of violent white flashes). This little Adamic figure with his *yeux méchants* sings *too* high, just as the Faun aimed too high in his Eros, resulting in a "sûr châtiment." The child will some day, no doubt, express this inner tendency with a more focussed act, a crime, that will cause him to lose his head through decapitation, related to castration as it clearly is in *Les Noces d'Hérodiade*.[2]

The *p*'s of *Pauvre* and *pâle* are a swelling "mushroom-cloud" of hubris – the "insolent" face, for example – as in the repeated *trop* of *Prose* (*pour des Esseintes*) connected with the *trop grand glaïeul* which was the key symbol of that major poem, where Mallarmé dealt with the excessive youthful vision which was his genius (genie exploding from a bottle) and near-demise. The *p* is a key tone of the work: compare "Pétal et papillon géants" and other such effects which I discuss in *Toward the Poems of Mallarmé*,[3] for example "en opposition trop pour" (*Coup de Dés*, page 7), expressing the lightning vision (and feather in his mad cap) of the Hamlet–poet.

The *u* of "tue-tête, rue, aigüe" is in an up–down tension parallel to that of *Le Démon de l'Analogie*, related powerfully to the theme of castration, decapitation, inversion: "coupant au ras les bonds . . . résume" (*Coup de Dés*, page 3).[4]

Is the *incarnadine* a hint of the bloody end (as Hérodiade's red-suffused cheeks were)?[5]

As-tu jamais eu un père? A likely source of genius and revenge in the image of Hamlet. The fatherless condition aggravates the sense of exile, alienation from a lost estate, the need for a coup to recover it.[6]

debout: he is projected upward like all Promethean urges; compare the "stature mignonne ténébreuse debout" (*Coup de Dés*, page 8), with its undertone *de boue*, its inversion in abeyance.

trop grand: recalling the observations on *trop* (and the *p*) earlier; he stands out beyond the other, more normal, children; dangerously . . .

Et ta complainte est si haute, si haute, que ta tête: a series of *t*'s have to do with the same vertical motif: "t: stationnement" (*Les Mots anglais*).[7] In *Le Nénuphar blanc*, Mallarmé fears to thrust his erotically curious head up too far: "n'est-ce, moi, tendre trop haut la tête . . . "

The *nue* links with the phallic and naked hubris theme, as in *Réminiscence*, the strikingly vertical body of the svelte and "naked" circus boy. There is a possibility of an overtone of *nue* as cloud (*en l'air*), a theme of breakaway from the body, as in *Saint Jean* and the essay on Banville: "s'en délivre, dans le voltige qu'il est seul" (p. 521). A cloud is detached in this sense in an early poem *Le Nuage*, as well as in the *Coup de Dés*, the Hamlet-feather: "voltige" (page 6). This leads to the idea of a head "taking off," *en décollant*, in a *décollation*.

A crime "isn't very difficult." The understanding of "There but for the grace of God go I" is present, as we noted earlier, and typical of Mallarmé.

The *jeûnes* of the last paragraph hints even at a sort of sinning saintliness, as in Flaubert, Mann, Dostoevsky *et al.* (*Legend of St Julian*, *The Holy Sinner*, *Crime and Punishment*). In the fragments of *Le Livre* there is a reference to the fasting artist, a theme picked up in the *Cantique de Saint Jean* and various fragments of *Les Noces d'Hérodiade*. One thinks naturally of Kafka's *The Hunger Artist* as well as the commonplace lore of *La Bohême* (*cf.* Mallarmé's *Le Guignon*).

The poet's sense of bourgeois guilt, unmerited and sterile safety (as in *Le Vierge, le vivace* – obliquely at least) is evident in "tu paieras pour moi, pour ceux qui valent moins que moi." As a poor struggling person – artist – himself, he puts himself in a sort of half-way position in this last phrase, but it is possible that the vagueness of his location *vis-à-vis* the window has to do with this ambiguity of his position and sympathy.

6

LA PIPE

⁊ **La Pipe**

Hier, j'ai trouvé ma pipe en rêvant une longue soirée de travail,
de beau travail d'hiver. Jetées les cigarettes avec toutes les joies
enfantines de l'été dans le passé qu'illuminent les feuilles bleues
de soleil, les mousselines et reprise ma grave pipe par un homme
sérieux qui veut fumer longtemps sans se déranger, afin de mieux
travailler: mais je ne m'attendais pas à la surprise que préparait
cette délaissée, à peine eus-je tiré la première bouffée, j'oubliai
mes grands livres à faire, émerveillé, attendri, je respirai l'hiver
dernier qui revenait. Je n'avais pas touché à la fidèle amie depuis
ma rentrée en France, et tout Londres, Londres tel que je le vécus
en entier à moi seul, il y a un an, est apparu; d'abord les chers
brouillards qui emmitouflent nos cervelles et ont, là-bas, une
odeur à eux, quand ils pénètrent sous la croisée. Mon tabac
sentait une chambre sombre aux meubles de cuir saupoudrés par
la poussière du charbon sur lesquels se roulait le maigre chat noir;
les grands feux! et la bonne aux bras rouges versant les charbons,
et le bruit de ces charbons tombant du seau de tôle dans la
corbeille de fer, le matin – alors que le facteur frappait le double
coup solennel, qui me faisait vivre! J'ai revu par les fenêtres ces
arbres malades du square désert – j'ai vu le large, si souvent
traversé cet hiver-là, grelottant sur le pont du steamer mouillé de
brume et noirci de fumée – avec ma pauvre bien-aimée errante, en
habits de voyageuse, une longue robe terne couleur de la poussière des routes, un manteau qui collait humide à ses épaules
froides, un de ces chapeaux de paille sans plume et presque sans
rubans, que les riches dames jettent en arrivant, tant ils sont
déchiquetés par l'air de la mer et que les pauvres bien-aimées
regarnissent pour bien des saisons encore. Autour de son cou
s'enroulait le terrible mouchoir qu'on agite en se disant adieu pour
toujours. ⋙

45

The Pipe

Yesterday I found my pipe while dreaming of a long evening of work, of fine winter work. The cigarettes thrown away with all the childish joys of summer into the past, which the leaves blue from the sun, the muslins, illuminate, and my grave pipe taken up again by a responsible man who wants to smoke for a long time without stirring, in order to work better: but I did not expect the surprise which this forsaken one was preparing, I had hardly drawn the first puff, when I forgot my great books to be written; amazed, softened, I inhaled last winter which was coming back. I had not touched the faithful friend since my return to France, and all of London, London as I lived it all for myself, a year ago, appeared; first the dear fogs which envelop our brains as if with a muff and have, over there, a smell of their own, when they seep under the casement-window. My tobacco smelled of a dark room with leather furniture sprinkled with coal dust on which the skinny black cat used to curl up; the big fires! and the maid with red arms pouring coals, and the noise of these coals falling from the sheet-iron bucket into the iron basket, in the morning – while the mailman gave his solemn double knock, which made me live! I saw again through the windows those sickly trees of the deserted square – I saw the open sea, crossed so often that winter, shivering on the steamer's deck soaked from the drizzle and grimy from smoke – with my poor wandering beloved in traveling clothes, a long faded dress the color of road dust, a coat that stuck damply to her cold shoulders, one of those straw hats with no feather and almost no ribbons, which the rich ladies throw away upon arrival, they are so frayed from the sea air and which poor loved ones refurbish for many a season more. Around her neck was wound the terrible kerchief which one waves when saying good-bye forever.

With Mallarmé, the tension – tetrapolar or polypolar – leading to (static) crystallization and (dynamic) rhythm and expression-in-time, such as writing, sound waves, and all the psychic analogies,[1] predominates so fiercely that his works, including the prose poems, are notably concise. The narrative aspect of the horizontal dimension tends to be foreshortened accordingly. Still, for example in *La Pipe*, the personal autobiographical narrative, combined with a perspective of travel in the background plus the broad city of London, is ample enough to provide excellent resistance to the poetic stance. The prose poem tone, in that respect, is quite ideal.

And the *frisson nouveau* that arose from Baudelaire's encounter of "sulking" self and reality, poet and city, is marvelously alive here. The shiver is also, overlappingly, a product of the shock of warm and cold, indoors and out, intimacy and the fog-bound expanse of London (represented closely by *la place*, the public *square*). The crystallization is like the one that occurs in Baudelaire's *Le Cygne*, arising from a tension of past and present, loss and love (which will become Proust's epiphanous memories).[2] It is the nostalgic resurrection, catalyzed by the puff on the pipe, of an anxious moment in Mallarmé's life when Marie, his fiancée, was teetering in and out of it, waving good-bye from a steamer crossing the Channel, in an atmosphere of savory uncertainty and perhaps peril: the tobacco aroma, "bitter and delicious as life" (Apollinaire) is linked to, and catalyzes the resurrection of, this hovering reality that is gradually crystallizing. It all comes back solidly, like the block of ice which stands for a poet's past in *Le Vierge, le vivace* – polypolar dream space ("le transparent glacier des vols qui n'ont pas fui")[3] – or Baudelaire's "rocks," palpably like the Japanese paper flower which was Combray rising, another Ys, from the cup of linden tea, with its houses, gardens, all.[4]

In *Frisson d'hiver* the shiver of the title is closely related, though it is less tense since the poet and his bride Marie (who *once*, upon a time, came from far away) are snugly together indoors.[5] Here too he is securely indoors, in winter, but the adventurous memory comes back with much of the power of *Brise marine*, a fancied flight to wild possibilities.

The "grave" pipe represents, amusingly to anyone older, a familiar attempt at maturity. It goes with newly-willed domestic duty, bread-earning for the incipient family, which was very much his need and mood at the time of writing this (1864; *cf. Don du Poème*). At this age he obviously talks himself into this seriousness,[6] perhaps overdoes it, for there is the backlash of poetic *involuntary* memory ...

Beau travail d'hiver: compare "l'hiver de l'art serein" (*Renouveau*, from roughly the same period). The outer-inflicted pain of cold stimulates good work, including poetic. *On connaît ça.*

The sunnily transparent, innocent "childish" joys of summer are fleetingly contrasted with this more adult phase of the pipe.[7] The tobacco ambivalence ("grave" delight) parallels the foggy, chilly joys of London with its "chers brouillards," "chambre sombre" and the warmth-bringing (in the form of dark coals) maid, the "steamer mouillé de brume et noirci de fumée";[8] and the *shiver* –

"grelottant sur le pont" – is, to repeat, of here–there, cold–warm, indoors–outdoors.

The suggested poverty of his *bien-aimée* is a similar source of tensely but tenderly ambivalent poetry, a vein Mallarmé had worked in some juvenilia such as *Galanterie macabre*. That note of loving pity colors *Don du Poème* as well. Marie, briefly, is at least a distant cousin of Mimi in *La Bohème*, even closer to Camus's Jeanne.[9]

The *facteur* brought news from Marie when she was on the other side of the Channel, at times, and he was clearly deeply attached to her; the news made him "live," as the early-lost mother did.

At the end the anxiety woven into delicious ambivalence is revealed as existential: the idea of never seeing someone again can easily arise in a departure, for a *cœur sans défense* such as his.

The *mouchoir* shows up again in *Brise marine*, as part of the familiar white imagery-chain.[10]

Windows – "croisée, les fenêtres" – are, again, very much a part of the framing of this piece, which is ideally shaped, physically, as a prose poem.

7

UN SPECTACLE
INTERROMPU

Mallarmé's genius, like Pascal's, touched "both extremes." The man was both eminently sane and daemonic. *Within* his (vertical, poetic) metaphoric axis there was a comparable tension, between the cult of punctilious form and utter freedom or wildness (or between idealism and the ground-breaking "materialism" Sartre saw, and so on). In this prose poem he coolly moves from one extreme to the other; with exemplary *sang-froid* he proposes a "miracle in the street" (Camus), a society of dreamers, sort of a surrealist club, plunk in the middle of a great modern city. And with the same unflappable aplomb he observes: "Artifice que la *réalité*, bon à fixer l'intellect moyen entre les mirages d'un fait."[1]

So he sets about giving us an example of what this visionary bunch would take as self-evident, a "type" of imposing dream–reality, in the same sense that ordinary rationalistic folk would take some commonplace as obviously real. And he finds one on the stage of a banal local theater.

This text, more than others in the collection, squares with the note of "Anecdote" which he sounded in the title. It is more narrative (like certain of the *Spleen de Paris* pieces), prosaic, longer. But there is poetry enough in its cosmic perspective foreshortened into a flash, and the bear, like the donkey of the medieval *fête de l'âne*, is, for just such reasons, a surefire hit, a born show stealer. Mallarmé feels right into him.

ೄ   **Un Spectacle interrompu**

Que la civilisation est loin de procurer les jouissances attribuables à cet état! on doit par exemple s'étonner qu'une association entre les rêveurs, y séjournant, n'existe pas, dans toute grande ville, pour subvenir à un journal qui remarque les événements sous le jour propre au rêve. Artifice que la *réalité*, bon à fixer l'intellect moyen entre les mirages d'un fait; mais elle repose par cela même sur quelque universelle entente: voyons donc s'il n'est pas, dans l'idéal, un aspect nécessaire, évident, simple, qui serve de type. Je veux, en vue de moi seul, écrire comme elle frappa mon regard de poëte, telle Anecdote, avant que la divulguent des *reporters* par la foule dressés à assigner à chaque chose son caractère commun.

Le petit théâtre des *PRODIGALITÉS* adjoint l'exhibition d'un vivant cousin d'Atta Troll ou de Martin à sa féerie classique la Bête et le Génie; j'avais, pour reconnaître l'invitation du billet double hier égaré chez moi, posé mon chapeau dans la stalle vacante à mes côtés, une absence d'ami y témoignait du goût général à esquiver ce naïf spectacle. Que se passait-il devant moi? rien, sauf que: de pâleurs évasives de mousseline se réfugiant sur vingt piédestaux en architecture de Bagdad, sortaient un sourire et des bras ouverts à la lourdeur triste de l'ours: tandis que le héros, de ces sylphides évocateur et leur gardien, un clown, dans sa haute nudité d'argent, raillait l'animal par notre supériorité. Jouir comme la foule du mythe inclus dans toute banalité, quel repos et, sans voisins où verser des réflexions, voir l'ordinaire et splendide veille trouvée à la rampe par ma recherche assoupie d'imaginations ou de symboles. Etranger à mainte réminiscence de pareilles soirées, l'accident le plus neuf! suscita mon attention: une des nombreuses salves d'applaudissements décernés selon l'enthousiasme à l'illustration sur la scène du privilège authentique de l'Homme, venait, brisée par quoi? de cesser net, avec un fixe fracas de gloire à l'apogée, inhabile à se répandre. Tout oreilles, il fallut être tout yeux. Au geste du pantin, une paume crispée dans l'air ouvrant les cinq doigts, je compris, qu'il avait, l'ingénieux! capté les sympathies par la mine d'attraper au vol quelque chose, figure (et c'est tout) de la facilité dont est par chacun prise une idée: et qu'ému au léger vent, l'ours rythmiquement et doucement levé interrogeait cet exploit, une griffe posée sur les rubans de l'épaule humaine. Personne qui ne haletât, tant cette situation portait de conséquences graves pour l'honneur de la race: qu'allait-il arriver? L'autre patte s'abattit, souple, contre un bras longeant le maillot; et l'on vit, couple uni dans un secret rapprochement, comme un homme inférieur, trapu, bon, debout sur l'écartement de deux jambes de poil, étreindre pour y apprendre les pratiques du génie, et son crâne au noir museau ne l'atteignant qu'à la moitié, le buste de son frère brillant et surnaturel: mais qui, lui! exhaussait, la bouche folle de vague, un chef affreux remuant par un fil visible dans l'horreur les dénégations véritables d'une mouche de papier et d'or. Spectacle clair, plus que les tréteaux vaste, avec ce don, propre à l'art, de durer longtemps: pour le parfaire je laissai, sans que m'offusquât l'attitude probablement fatale prise par le mime dépositaire de notre orgueil, jaillir tacitement le discours interdit au rejeton des sites arctiques: "Sois bon (c'était le sens), et plutôt que.de manquer à la charité, explique-moi la vertu de cette atmosphère de splendeur, de poussière et de voix, où tu m'appris à me mouvoir. Ma requête, pressante, est juste, que tu ne sembles pas, en une angoisse qui n'est que feinte, répondre ne savoir, élancé aux régions de la sagesse, aîné subtil! à moi, pour te faire libre, vêtu encore du séjour informe des cavernes où je replongeai, dans la nuit d'époques humbles ma force latente. Authentiquons, par cette embrassade étroite, devant la multitude siégeant à cette fin, le pacte de notre réconciliation." L'absence d'aucun souffle unie à l'espace, dans quel lieu absolu vivais-je, un des drames de l'histoire astrale élisant, pour s'y produire, ce modeste théâtre! La foule s'effaçait, toute, en l'emblème de sa situation spirituelle magnifiant la scène: dispensateur moderne de l'extase, seul, avec l'impartialité d'une chose élémentaire, le gaz, dans les hauteurs de la salle, continuait un bruit lumineux d'attente.

Le charme se rompit: c'est quand un morceau de chair, nu, brutal, traversa ma vision dirigé de l'intervalle des décors, en avance de quelques instants sur la récompense, mystérieuse d'ordinaire après ces représentations. Loque substituée saignant auprès de l'ours qui, ses instincts retrouvés antérieurement à une curiosité plus haute dont le dotait le rayonnement théâtral, retomba à quatre pattes et, comme emportant parmi soi le Silence, alla de la marche étouffée de l'espèce, flairer, pour y appliquer les dents, cette proie. Un soupir, exempt presque de déception, soulagea incompréhensiblement l'assemblée: dont les lorgnettes, par rangs, cherchèrent, allumant la netteté de leurs verres, le jeu du splendide imbécile évaporé dans sa peur; mais virent un repas abject préféré peut-être par l'animal à la même chose qu'il lui eût fallu d'abord faire de *notre image*, pour y goûter. La toile, hésitant jusque-là à accroître le danger ou l'émotion, abattit subitement son journal de tarifs et de lieux communs. Je me levai comme tout le monde, pour aller respirer au dehors, étonné de n'avoir pas senti, cette fois encore, le même genre d'impression que mes semblables, mais serein: car ma façon de voir, après tout, avait été supérieure, et même la vraie.　　　◈

51

≿ **An Interrupted Performance**

How far civilization is from procuring the enjoyments attributable to that state! it is surprising, for example, that there exists no association of dreamers living in every big city, to support a journal observing events in the light peculiar to dreams. An artifice, *reality*, is good for fixing the average intellect in the mirages of a fact; but it rests by that very situation on some universal understanding: let us see, then, if there is not, in the ideal, a necessary, evident, simple aspect, which might serve as a type. I want to write, for the benefit of myself alone, a certain Anecdote, as it struck my poet's gaze, before *reporters*, set up by the crowd to assign each thing its common character, divulge it.

The little theatre of the PRODIGALITÉS adds the exhibition of a living cousin of Atta Troll or Martin to its classic fairy tale, *The Beast and the Genius*; I had, in order to acknowledge the invitation of the double ticket yesterday strayed to my house, placed my hat in the empty seat at my side, a friend's absence there bearing witness to a general taste for avoiding this naive show. What was happening in front of me? nothing, except that from evasive palenesses of muslin taking refuge on twenty pedestals of Bagdad style, a smile and open arms were going out to the bear's sad heaviness; while the hero, the conjuror and protector of these sylphs, a clown, in his tall, silver nakedness, was taunting the animal by our superiority. To enjoy like the crowd the myth enclosed in every banality, what a relaxation for the mind and, without neighbors to whom to pour out reflections, to behold the ordinary and splendid vigil found at the footlights by my lulled quest of imaginings or symbols. Foreign to many a recollection of similar evenings, the most novel accident! aroused my attention: one of the numerous salvos of applause bestowed according to the enthusiasm for Man's authentic privilege illustrated on the stage, had, broken by what? just come to a dead stop, with a fixed din of glory at the peak, unable to spread. All ears, one had to be all eyes. At the puppet's gesture, a fist clenched in the air opening its five fingers, I understood that he, the ingenious one, had won the sympathies by the appearance of catching something in flight, a figure (and that is all) of the ease with which an idea is taken up by everyone: and that, set in motion by the light breeze, the bear, risen rhythmically and gently, was interrogating this exploit, one claw placed on the ribbons of the human shoulder. No one who did not breathe hard, such grave consequences did this situation bear for the honor of the race: what

52

was going to happen? The other paw came down, supple, against the arm hanging against the tights; and one saw, a couple united in a secret coming-together, something like an inferior, squat, and good man, standing on two spread-out, furry legs, embrace, in order to learn there the practices of genius, and his skull with the black muzzle only half reaching it, the bust of his brilliant and supernatural brother: but who! himself was raising, his mouth crazy with vagueness, a frightful head moving by a thread visible in the horror the true denials of a paper and gold fly. Bright spectacle, vaster than the stage, with this gift, proper to art, of lasting for a long time: in order to complete it, I let, without being shocked by the probably fatal attitude taken on by the mime, the depository of our pride, tacitly pour forth the discourse forbidden to the descendant of arctic sites: "Be kind (that was the meaning), and rather than be wanting in charity, explain to me the quality of this atmosphere of splendor, of dust and voices, in which you have taught me to move. My urgent request is just, which you do not seem, in an anguish which is only feigned, to not know how to answer, launched into the regions of wisdom, subtle elder! me, in order to make you free, still dressed in the crude abode of the caves where I have plunged again, in the night of humble epochs, my latent strength. Let us authenticate, by this tight embrace, before the multitude assembled for this purpose, the pact of our reconciliation." The absence of any breath united to space, in what absolute place was I living, one of the dramas of astral history choosing, in order to produce itself there, this modest stage! The crowd was fading away completely, magnifying the stage as the emblem of its spiritual situation: modern dispenser of ecstasy, the gas, alone, with the impartiality of an elemental thing, was continuing, in the heights of the hall, a luminous noise of expectation.

The spell was broken: it was when a naked, brutal piece of flesh, guided from the space between the stage settings, crossed my vision, some moments in advance of the usually mysterious reward after these performances. A rag substituted, bleeding, near the bear who, having rediscovered his instincts previous to a higher curiosity with which the theatrical radiance was endowing him, fell back on his four paws and, as if carrying the Silence away with him, went with the muted step of the species to scent, in order to put his teeth to it, this prey. A sigh, almost exempt of disappointment, incomprehensible relieved the assembly: whose opera glasses, in rows, sought, lighting up the clarity of their lenses, the acting of the splendid imbecile evaporated in his fear; but saw an abject meal preferred perhaps by the animal to the same thing which it would first have been necessary for him to make of *our image*, in order to enjoy it. The curtain having hesitated until then to increase the danger or the emotion, suddenly lowered its announcements of prices and commonplaces. I got up like everyone else, to go outside and take a breath of air, astonished not to have felt, once again, the same kind of impression as my fellow man, but serene: for my way of seeing, after all, had been superior, and even the true one. ◄§

First, he gently puts down the "naïf spectacle": twenty "sylphides" on pedestals smiling from amidst their pale muslin at a clumsy bear,[2] being mocked by the "hero," a clown, standing up tall like a single male principle amongst that feminine plurality[3] ("dans sa haute nudité d'argent" echoes the svelte circus boy in his *maillot*, in *Réminiscence*). The clown maintaining "notre supériorité" over the primitive creature is an example of the "mythe inclus dans toute banalité" – for those with cultured eyes to see – a simple rite of man *versus* beast. Mallarmé finds this restful and lets his usual symbol-hunting imagination go to sleep as he enjoys the "ordinary and splendid awakedness," the sensationally lighted space of mere spectacle.

Then something unprecedented happens, an "accident" unlike – "étranger" to – many remembrances of similar theater evenings. A salvo of applause stimulated by the illustration of human privilege up there breaks off abruptly, suspending itself in mid-air, as it were, unable to go on ("se répande"). What happened? From listening (to the applause) he now turned to looking intently.

The clown had been imitating a fly-catching gesture with his hand, and the bear, fascinated, had put his heavy paw on his shoulder; then, another paw descended against one downward-dangling arm of the clown, in a sort of incipient bear-hug. He seemed to be trying to learn the secrets of human "genius." But the clown, terrified, waving his head in (symbolic) denial,[4] moves therewith (really) the gilded paper imitation fly that was attached to his noggin by a string (plus, no doubt, some kind of wand fixed on the clownhead).

Mallarmé sees this spectacle as "clair" and vaster than the little stage, durable as art is, exuding a universal truth worth preserving.[5]

He imagines the bear speaking (and here I paraphrase)[6]

Be good ... and rather than lack charity, explain to me the virtue (or meaning) of this atmosphere of splendor, dust, and voices in which you taught me to move. My pressing request is just, which (request) you – only feignedly anguished – don't seem unable to reply to me – raised up (as you are) to the regions of wonder, subtle older brother (to me) who in order to make you free (am, by contrast) still dressed in the formless habit of the caves where I replunged my latent force in the night of humble epochs. Let us authenticate, through this close embrace, before the multitude seated here for the reason, the fact of our reconciliation.

This stilted style hardly suits the bear, but what style does? Colette, Ravel (in *L'Enfant et les sortilèges*) had their creatures speak in stunted, half-muffled tones. Since Mallarmé's complex prose manner *descends* towards the structure of the cosmos even as it aspires upward, in a way it is appropriate to put it into the mouth of the simple bear, on this extreme-reconciling – *justement* – metaphorical plane.

l'absence d'aucun souffle: everybody stops breathing. The crowd disappears, as it were, into the significant event on the stage. Only the gas-jet still makes any noise.[7]

A chunk of raw meat is thrown from the wings, to distract the bear. In "traversa ma vision," the phenomenological style, undecidably between subject and object, gives the event immediacy. This whole piece is masterly in this sense, with a stunning precision in the way the bear is described.

A sigh, which incomprehensibly, to Mallarmé, shows no disappointment (at having the drama curtailed), emerges from the public. The hero is described as a "splendid imbecile evaporated in his fear." Clearly Mallarmé sides largely with the bear, despising such cruel mockery *de haut en bas* as Baudelaire did in his prose poem, *Un plaisant*, where a "magnifique imbécile, qui me parut concentrer en lui tout l'esprit de la France" baits a poor donkey. The meat replaces the meat or flesh of the clown, "notre image," in Mallarmé's biting phrase. Here we have the same sort of fluid reversibility that occurred in *Pauvre Enfant pâle*.[8]

The curtain comes down (having waited till the danger of its aggravating the bear had passed) with its usual advertisements, just the kind of "lieux communs" which constitute the reality he had found insufficient *ab initio*. And he ends by reaffirming the value of *his* way of seeing things, surprised (is he really?) that others did not share it.

This way of apprehending the relation between man and beast during the privileged moment – "un des drames de l'histoire astrale" – is structurally relevant to Mallarmé's central vision as he developed it tentatively in the fragments of *Le Livre*. Here we find just such a confrontation: animals, representing various motifs of elementary structure (circles, lines, white, black) combine in various manoeuvers and hybrid metamorphoses, showing how reality develops. At one point they draw back, as creatures do before human fires and just as the bear does here, failing to "make it" toward an appropriation of the divine spark which would enable them to rise on the scale of evolution.

The *Coup de Dés* transfers these motifs to ocean waves, simpler nature, in a move toward adequacy and poetic purification. Animals are too specific, *anecdotal*, exotic as they are in zoos or circuses, for such use.[9] But since we are dealing here with an "Anecdote,"[10] precisely, Mallarmé shows his virtuosity on this terrain too.

We note that this is the first of the *Derniers poëmes*, and that the late style is tried out experimentally, as it were, on the bear, at its most *contourné* or *amphigourique*. The whole piece moves gingerly in this direction. The next one goes full steam ahead.

8
RÉMINISCENCE

↜   **Réminiscence**

Orphelin, j'errais en noir et l'œil vacant de famille: au quinconce
se déplièrent des tentes de fête, éprouvai-je le futur et que je serais
ainsi, j'aimais le parfum des vagabonds, vers eux à oublier mes
camarades. Aucun cri de chœurs par la déchirure, ni tirade loin, le
drame requérant l'heure sainte des quinquets, je souhaitais de
parler avec un môme trop vacillant pour figurer parmi sa race, au
bonnet de nuit taillé comme le chaperon de Dante; qui rentrait en
soi, sous l'aspect d'une tartine de fromage mou, déjà la neige des
cimes, le lys ou autre blancheur constitutive d'ailes au-dedans: je
l'eusse prié de m'admettre à son repas supérieur, partagé vite avec
quelque aîné fameux jailli contre une proche toile en train des tours
de force et banalités alliables au jour. Nu, de pirouetter dans sa
prestesse de maillot à mon avis surprenante, lui, qui d'ailleurs
commença: "Tes parents? – Je n'en ai pas. – Allons, si tu savais
comme c'est farce, un père . . . même l'autre semaine que bouda la
soupe, il faisait des grimaces aussi belles, quand le maître lançait les
claques et les coups de pied. Mon cher!" et de triompher en élevant
à moi la jambe avec aisance glorieuse, "il nous épate, papa," puis
de mordre au régal chaste du très jeune: "Ta maman, tu n'en as pas
peut-être, que tu es seul? la mienne mange de la filasse et le monde
bat des mains. Tu ne sais rien, des parents sont des gens drôles, qui
font rire." La parade s'exaltait, il partit: moi, je soupirai, déçu
tout-à-coup de n'avoir pas de parents.   ❧

↜   **Reminiscence**

An orphan, I was wandering, in black and my eye vacant of family;
at the quincunx tents of a fair were unfolded; did I experience the
future and that I would be like that? I loved the scent of the
vagabonds, drawn toward them forgetting my companions. No cry

57

of the chorus through the gash, nor distant tirade, the drama requiring the holy hour of the footlights, I wanted to speak to an urchin too wobbly to appear among his people, with a nightcap cut like Dante's hood; who was putting inside himself, in the form of a slice of bread with soft cheese, already the snow of the mountain peaks, the lily or other whiteness constituting wings within: I would have begged him to admit me to his superior meal, quickly shared with some illustrious elder suddenly sprung up against a nearby tent, engaged in feats of strength and banalities compatible with the day. Naked, he pirouetted in the to me surprising nimbleness of his tights and began moreover: "Your parents? – I do not have any. – Go on, if you knew how funny that is, a father ... even the other week when he was off his food, he made faces just as beautiful as ever, when the boss was distributing slaps and kicks. My dear fellow!" and he triumphed raising his leg toward me with glorious ease, "he amazes us, papa," then he bit into the chaste meal of the very young one: "Your mom, perhaps you don't have one, you're alone? mine eats tow, and everybody claps their hands. You have no idea, parents are funny people, who make one laugh." The parade was rising to excitement, he left: I sighed, disappointed suddenly not to have parents.   ⚜

Here is another little orphaned Hamlet-figure, "en noir." This one is wandering, looking for a father–principle to fix his life and give it orientation, one senses. Baudelaire, in a stirring prose poem, *Le Vieux saltimbanque*, saw his future self in a wretched old circus performer. Early on, Mallarmé, in the wake of Poe, identified with the "mauvais Hamlet" who was a clown, a *pitre*, so it is not surprising that he too, looking back – "Réminiscence" – could see a future in this direction, whether self-derisively (as in *Le Pitre châtié* and the correspondence of that period) or, in a positive sense, the kind of semi-artistry, exhibitionism, prowess and adventure represented by a circus, as it would for Picasso, Cocteau, Satie, etc.

So many fatherless boys, with much to prove, become bullfighters for similar reasons, in Hispanic lands.[1] Nothing this demanding is sought or found here, but still the small quester is stunned by the lightning-stroke, phallic or vertical, svelte ("nu ... dans sa prestesse de maillot") apparition of an adolescent acrobat against a tent wall. *De ce côté-là ...*

At the outset, the eye of the vagrant child is "vacant de famille," which succinctly tells of his orphaned state and also implies no interest in ordinary bourgeois family life. But this circus family excites his envy, aggravates his feeling of abandonment. It is like those changeling fantasies which beset many sensitive children as they near puberty: it must be that a wicked fairy snatched us from the royalty we were born to ... As the adolescent gets needy and questing enough, he sets out looking for that august ancestry, a bit like that Old Testament scion who went looking for his father's banal asses and found a kingdom. Little Marcel eyed the stained-glass King in the church at Combray, or the Duchesse de Guermantes in her inaccessible pew, in that spirit. It is an old theme of quiet childhood desperation and faëry. Some run away to join a circus, or at least send their hearts.

The identification – "je serais ainsi" – reminds us somewhat of the *Montreur* as a minor surrogate of the artist in *Le Phénomène futur*, or Mallarmé's role as barker in *La Déclaration foraine*: he seems to have enjoyed playing master of ceremonies on trivial social occasions, commemorated in some *vers de circonstance*.

The small circus boy he first encounters – slightly echoing fatherless questing Perceval and the damsel with the pie – is stuffing a *tartine* into himself, and one admires the accurate memory of childhood here, with its steep envies! The cheese-covered bread "takes off" into infinite vistas along the whiteness-chain: "déjà la neige des cimes, le lys ou autre blancheur constitutive d'ailes au-dedans." Those wings can be compared seriously to the ones beating toward the ideal in Plato's *Phaedrus*, an ideal as rhapsodically, drunkenly sensual as Mallarmé's or the equally "drunk" wing-beat of *Le Vierge, le vivace*; or the transparent sunlit grape-skins stared through to the Source in the *Faune*, "avid for drunkenness."

In the early version printed in an appendix to this chapter, we read that the orphan wanderer had lowered his eyes from the skies and sought his family on the earth. This is an anti-idealist and existential note of the sort that gratified Sartre in his study of Mallarmé. But, as in *L'Azur* the old ideal beauty stabs back past his defenses, through the cheese *tartine*! No one is more modern than Mallarmé; those who dub him "Platonist" in the sense of one-sided idealism are, as Sartre flatly said, "dupes or knaves."[2]

This prose poem, though first written in 1864, was extensively reworked before being printed in its final version in 1891. Its difficulties are not forbidding, but it is well on its way to later Mallarmé in style. Norman Paxton, in his *The Development of Mallarmé's Prose Style* (Paris: Droz, 1968) gives a reliable account of how this comes about, in general.

quinconce: French towns often have one for market areas, *foires*, *fêtes foraines*. It is echoed tantalizingly by the *quinquets* (Argand lamps) a few lines down. This *quin* may just have some bearing on the five-part structure of the first sentence.[3] Even more incidentally, the two accents on *déplièrent* as well as the similarly shaped circumflex of *fête*, seem pleasantly to reflect a tent shape.

Aucun cri: It's too early for the show, which awaits the *quinquet* hour.

un môme trop vacillant . . . chaperon de Dante: the real stuff of childhood and its mysterious encounters. Rimbaud will go no further in this plunge and intimacy. The cheese *tartine* is just as real and intimate.

banalités alliables au jour: mild *tours*, in the mere daytime, warming up.

This prestigious ephebe is ingrained in earth and life. He knows hunger, "une réalité rugueuse" (Rimbaud). But it is "bitter and delicious," to use Apollinaire again. Even when hungry, the adored father clowned it up just as lustily.

The virtuoso ease of the lifted leg is all the prestige of the *older boy*; Meaulnes dazzled François Seurel with his ability to handle fireworks or hunt for marsh-hens' eggs. Those older boys are mediating figures *par excellence*, on the way to the full father image. At the end the fête is beginning to stir toward the evening activity, in three choice words: "la parade s'exaltait."

Eluard loved this piece. Picasso came to Paris largely because of Mallarmé, according to Henri Peyre.[4] I like to think this item had something to do with that pilgrimage.

APPENDIX

From the Pléiade edition of the *Œuvres* we learn that this piece was originally called *L'Orphelin*. Written in 1864, it first appeared under that title in 1867, in the *Revue des Lettres et des Arts*, in a quite different version. The one printed here appeared in *Pages*, in 1891, then in *Divagations*.

The style changed interestingly, according to the typical patterns of the evolving Mallarmé: more ellipse, more succinct accuracy, and the like. The whiteness-chain was more extensive: "les lys ravis, la neige, la plume des cygnes, les étoiles, et toutes les blancheurs sacrées des poëtes . . ."

"Orphelin . . . les yeux baissés du ciel et cherchant ma famille sur la terre" indicates the well-known religious crisis which we follow in the correspondence. And there are other fascinating details. The text follows.

L'Orphelin

Orphelin, déjà, enfant avec tristesse pressentant le Poëte, j'errais vêtu de noir, les yeux baissés du ciel et cherchant ma famille sur la terre. Une fois s'arrêtèrent sous les arbres dont le vent cassait le bois mort, près de la rivière, des baraques de foire. Devinais-je ma parenté et que je serais des leurs, plus tard, mais j'aimais à vivre de la vie de ces comédiens et vers eux j'allais oublier mes hideux camarades. Par les planches m'arrivaient, brise ancienne des chœurs, des voix d'enfant maudissant un tyran, avec de grêles tirades, car Thalie habitait la tente et attendait l'heure sainte des quinquets. Je rôdais devant ces tréteaux, orgueilleux, et plus trem-blant de la pensée de parler à un enfant trop jeune pour jouer parmi ses frères, mais qui s'appuyait au cintre des toiles écarlates de pourpoints et d'audace romantique, peintes par le maître qui, peut-être, à cet instant, croyait seul au moyen âge. L'enfant, je le vois toujours, coiffé d'un bonnet de nuit taillé comme le chaperon du Dante, mangeait, sous la forme d'une tartine de fromage blanc, les lys ravis, la neige, la plume des cygnes, les étoiles, et toutes les blancheurs sacrées des poëtes: je l'eusse bien prié de m'admettre à son repas si je n'avais été si timide, mais il le partagea avec un autre qui vint brusquement, en sautant, – un petit saltimbanque de la baraque voisine dans laquelle on allait donner les tours de force, ce frivole exercice ne se refusant pas à la banalité du grand jour. Il était tout nu dans un maillot lavé et pirouettait avec une tur-bulence surprenante: ce fut lui qui m'adressa la parole: "Où sont tes parents? – Je n'en ai pas, lui dis-je. – Ah! tu n'as pas de père, moi, j'en ai un. Si tu savais comme c'est amusant un père, ça rit toujours ... même l'autre soir où l'on a mis en terre mon petit frère, il faisait des grimaces plus belles quand le maître lui lançait des claques et des coups de pied. Mon cher, dit-il, en élevant sa jambe disloquée avec une facilité glorieuse, il m'amuse bien, papa." Puis il mordit encore dans la tartine du plus jeune enfant qui ne parlait pas. "Et de maman, tu n'en as donc pas non plus, que tu es tout seul? La mienne mange de la filasse et tout le monde tape des mains. Tu ne connais pas cela, toi. – Voilà, des parents sont des gens drôles qui nous font rire." Mais sa parade venait de commencer, et il partit après ces mots. Moi, je m'en allai tout seul, songeant que c'était bien triste que je n'eusse pas comme lui des parents.

Another early title Mallarmé thought of was *Le Petit saltimbanque*, which seems to echo the Baudelaire work, *Le Vieux saltimbanque*. Still another title he toyed with: *Le Môme sagace*.

9

LA DÉCLARATION FORAINE

Mallarmé (i.e. the narrator), out riding in a landau, with his lady friend of a late afternoon melting into evening, is invited by her to stop in at a fair. She, seeing an inactive sideshow booth, impulsively asks the unoccupied tenant to beat his drum and attract a crowd. The offered exhibition is "merely" her vivid beauty standing on a table. Mallarmé, feeling constrained to explain to the puzzled onlookers what they are getting, recites an exceedingly complex – even for him – sonnet, celebrating the woman's intrinsic glory, and especially that of her hair. We are made to feel that this somehow satisfies them. Then everyone departs.

This is a more sophisticated version of *Le Phénomène futur*, with "Mallarmé" replacing the *Montreur* and present substituting for future. And this time the featured beauty is not naked, though her flaming hair is, flaring into consciousness. It is the main event. Her chic clothes also get into the act.

La Déclaration foraine is incomparably tighter in texture than the preceding pieces. Counterpointed meanings, ambiguities, overtones, are rife. We shall have to go through it line by line.

ৡ৶ **La Déclaration foraine**

Le Silence! il est certain qu'à mon côté, ainsi que songes, étendue dans un bercement de promenade sous les roues assoupissant l'interjection de fleurs, toute femme, et j'en sais une qui voit clair ici, m'exempte de l'effort à proférer un vocable: la complimenter haut de quelque interrogatrice toilette, offre de soi presque à l'homme en faveur de qui s'achève l'après-midi, ne pouvant à l'encontre de tout ce rapprochement fortuit, que suggérer la distance sur ses traits aboutie à une fossette de spirituel sourire. Ainsi ne consent la réalité; car ce fut impitoyablement, hors du rayon qu'on sentait avec luxe expirer aux vernis du landau, comme une vocifération, parmi trop de tacite félicité pour une tombée de

63

jour sur la banlieue, avec orage, dans tous sens à la fois et sans motif, du rire strident ordinaire des choses et de leur cuivrerie triomphale: au fait, la cacophonie à l'ouïe de quiconque, un instant écarté, plutôt qu'il ne s'y fond, auprès de son idée, reste à vif devant la hantise de l'existence.

"La fête de . . ." et je ne sais quel rendez-vous suburbain! nomma l'enfant voiturée dans mes distractions, la voix claire d'aucun ennui; j'obéis et fis arrêter.

Sans compensation à cette secousse qu'un besoin d'explication figurative plausible pour mes esprits, comme symétriquement s'ordonnent des verres d'illumination peu à peu éclairés en guirlandes et attributs, je décidai, la solitude manquée, de m'enfoncer même avec bravoure en ce déchaînement exprès et haïssable de tout ce que j'avais naguère fui dans une gracieuse compagnie: prête et ne témoignant de surprise à la modification dans notre programme, du bras ingénu elle s'en repose sur moi, tandis que nous allons parcourir, les yeux sur l'enfilade, l'allée d'ahurissement qui divise en écho du même tapage les foires et permet à la foule d'y renfermer pour un temps l'univers. Subséquemment aux assauts d'un médiocre dévergondage en vue de quoi que ce soit qui détourne notre stagnation amusée par la crépuscule, au fond, bizarre et pourpre, nous retint à l'égal de la nue incendiaire un humain spectacle, poignant: reniée du châssis peinturluré ou de l'inscription en capitales une baraque, apparemment vide.

A qui ce matelas décousu pour improviser ici, comme les voiles dans tous les temps et les temples, l'arcane! appartînt, sa fréquentation durant le jeûne n'avait pas chez son possesseur excité avant qu'il le déroulât comme le gonfalon d'espoirs en liesse, l'hallucination d'une merveille à montrer (que l'inanité de son famélique cauchemar); et pourtant, mû par le caractère frérial d'exception à la misère quotidienne qu'un pré, quand l'institue le mot mystérieux de fête, tient des souliers nombreux y piétinant (en raison de cela poind aux profondeurs des vêtements quelque unique velléité du dur sou à sortir à seule fin de se dépenser), lui aussi! n'importe qui de tout dénué sauf de la notion qu'il y avait lieu pour être un des élus, sinon de vendre, de faire voir, mais quoi, avait cédé à la convocation du bienfaisant rendez-vous. Ou, très prosaïquement, peut-être le rat éduqué à moins que, lui-même, ce mendiant sur l'athlétique vigueur de ses muscles comptât, pour décider l'engouement populaire, faisait défaut, à l'instant précis, comme cela résulte souvent de la mise en demeure de l'homme par les circonstances générales.

"Battez la caisse!" proposa en altesse Madame ... seule tu sais Qui, marquant un suranné tambour duquel se levait, les bras décroisés afin de signifier inutile l'approche de son théâtre sans prestige, un vieillard que cette camaraderie avec un instrument de rumeur et d'appel, peut-être, séduisit à son vacant dessein; puis comme si, de ce que tout de suite on pût, ici, envisager de plus beau, l'énigme, par un bijou fermant la mondaine, en tant qu'à sa gorge le manque de réponse, scintillait! la voici engouffrée, à ma surprise de pitre coi devant une halte du public qu'empaume l'éveil des ra et des fla assourdissant mon invariable et obscur pour moi-même d'abord. "Entrez, tout le monde, ce n'est qu'un sou, on le rend à qui n'est pas satisfait de la présentation." Le nimbe en paillasson dans le remerciement joignant deux paumes séniles vidé, j'en agite les couleurs, en signal, de loin, et me coiffai, prêt à fendre la masse debout en le secret de ce qu'avait su faire avec ce lieu sans rêve l'initiative d'une contemporaine de nos soirs.

A hauteur du genou, elle émergeait, sur une table, des cent têtes.

Net ainsi qu'un jet égaré d'autre part la dardait électriquement, éclate pour moi ce calcul qu'à défaut de tout, elle, selon que la mode, une fantaisie ou l'humeur du ciel circonstanciaient sa beauté, sans supplément de danse ou de chant, pour la cohue amplement payait l'aumône exigée en faveur d'un quelconque; et du même trait je comprends mon devoir en le péril de la subtile exhibition, ou qu'il n'y avait au monde pour conjurer la défection dans les curiosités que de recourir à quelque puissance absolue, comme d'une Métaphore. Vite, dégoiser jusqu'à éclaircissement, sur maintes physionomies, de leur sécurité qui, ne saisissant tout du coup, se rend à l'évidence, même ardue, impliquée en la parole et consent à échanger son billon contre des présomptions exactes et supérieures, bref, la certitude pour chacun de n'être pas refait.

Un coup d'œil, le dernier, à une chevelure où fume puis éclaire de fastes de jardins le pâlissement du chapeau en crêpe de même ton que la statuaire robe se relevant, avance au spectateur, sur pied comme le reste hortensia.

Alors:

> La chevelure vol d'une flamme à l'extrême
> Occident de désirs pour la tout déployer
> Se pose (je dirais mourir un diadème)
> Vers le front couronné son ancien foyer
>
> Mais sans or soupirer que cette vive nue
> L'ignition du feu toujours intérieur
> Originellement la seule continue
> Dans le joyau de l'œil véridique ou rieur

Une nudité de héros tendre diffame
Celle qui ne mouvant astre ni feux au doigt
Rien qu'à simplifier avec gloire la femme
Accomplit par son chef fulgurante l'exploit

De semer de rubis le doute qu'elle écorche
Ainsi qu'une joyeuse et tutélaire torche.

Mon aide à la taille de la vivante allégorie qui déjà résignait sa faction, peut-être faute chez moi de faconde ultérieure, afin d'en assoupir l'élan gentiment à terre: "Je vous ferai observer, ajoutai-je, maintenant de plain-pied avec l'entendement des visiteurs, coupant court à leur ébahissement devant ce congé par une affection de retour à l'authenticité du spectacle, Messieurs et Dames, que la personne qui a eu l'honneur de se soumettre à votre jugement, ne requiert pour vous communiquer le sens de son charme, un costume ou aucun accessoire usuel du théâtre. Ce naturel s'accommode de l'allusion parfaite que fournit la toilette toujours à l'un des motifs primordiaux de la femme, et suffit, ainsi que votre sympathique approbation m'en convainc." Un suspens de marque appréciative sauf quelques confondants "Bien sûr!" ou "C'est cela!" et "Oui" par les gosiers comme plusieurs bravos prêtés par des paires de mains généreuses, conduisit jusqu'à la sortie sur une vacance d'arbres et de nuit la foule où nous allions nous mêler, n'était l'attente en gants blancs encore d'un enfantin tourlourou qui les rêvait dégourdir à l'estimation d'une jarretière hautaine.

– Merci, consentit la chère, une bouffée droit à elle d'une constellation ou des feuilles bue comme pour y trouver sinon le rassérènement, elle n'avait douté d'un succès, du moins l'habitude frigide de sa voix: j'ai dans l'esprit le souvenir de choses qui ne s'oublient.

– Oh! rien que lieu commun d'une esthétique . . .

– Que vous n'auriez peut-être pas introduit, qui sait? mon ami, le prétexte de formuler ainsi devant moi au conjoint isolement par exemple de notre voiture – où est-elle – regagnons-la: – mais ceci jaillit, forcé, sous le coup de poing brutal à l'estomac, que cause une impatience de gens auxquels coûte que coûte et soudain il faut proclamer quelque chose fût-ce la rêverie . . .

– Qui s'ignore et se lance nue de peur, en travers du public; c'est vrai. Comme vous, Madame, ne l'auriez entendu si irréfutablement, malgré sa réduplication sur une rime du trait final, mon boniment d'après un mode primitif du sonnet, je le gage, si chaque terme ne s'en était répercuté jusqu'à vous par de variés tympans, pour charmer un esprit ouvert à la compréhension multiple.

–Peut-être! accepta notre pensée dans un enjouement de souffle nocturne la même. ◄§

The Declaration at a Fair

Silence! it is certain that by my side, like dreams, in the lulling swaying of the ride, under the wheels, veiling the interjection of flowers, any woman, and I know of one who clearly sees this, excuses me from the effort of uttering a word: to compliment her aloud on some questioning costume, almost an offer of herself to the man in whose favor the afternoon draws to a close, contrary to all this fortuitous conjunction of circumstances awaiting only to suggest the distance which ends on her features in the dimple of an intelligent smile. Reality does not allow it so; for there was mercilessly, outside the sunbeam which one felt expiring luxuriously on the landau's varnish, something like an outcry, amongst too much tacit bliss for a nightfall on the outskirts of town, stormily, everywhere at the same time and without reason, of the shrill common laughter of things and their triumphal brassiness: in fact, the cacophony to the ears of whoever, having withdrawn for a moment near his idea, rather than melting into it, remains open to the obsession of existence.

"The fair of ..." and I do not know what sort of suburban rendez-vous! indicated the girl-child transported in my distractions, with her clear voice devoid of dismay; I obeyed and ordered a stop.

Without compensation for this shock except a need for a figurative explanation plausible to my mind, like lamps, lit up little by little, which arrange themselves symmetrically in garlands and emblems, I decided, having lost solitude, to plunge, with daring even, into this express and detestable outburst of all that I had lately fled in gracious company: ready, and showing no surprise at our change in our plans, she relies on me with ingenuous arm while we go down, our eyes upon the enfilade, the lane of confusion which divides fairs into an echo of the same din and permits the crowd to enclose in for a time the universe. Subsequent to the onslaughts of a mediocre licentiousness with a view to anything whatever which diverts our stagnation entertained by the dusk, as much as the incendiary cloud in the background, strange and purple, a heart-gripping human spectacle detained us: a shanty, apparently empty repudiated by the garish frame or the inscription in capital letters.

To whomsoever belonged this mattress ripped apart in order to improvise here, like the veils in all times and temples, mystery! its frequentation during his fast had not excited in its possessor before he unrolled it as the banner of gay hopes, the hallucination of a marvel to show (except the inanity of his famished nightmare); and yet, stirred by the fraternal character of exception to daily misery which a meadow, when the mysterious word "fair" institutes it, derives from numerous shoes trampling on it (for this reason dawns in the depths of clothes some unique whim of the hard penny to come out for the sole purpose of being spent) he too! anyone at all, destitute of all except the notion that there it was incumbent in order to be one of the elect, if not to sell, then to show, but what? had yielded to the summons of the beneficent rendezvous. Or, very prosaically, perhaps the trained rat, unless the beggar himself was counting on the athletic vigor of his muscles, to determine the popular craze, was at the precise moment absent, as often results from man's summons by general circumstances.

"Beat the drum!" proposed haughtily Madame ... you alone know Who, pointing to an old-fashioned drum whence rose, his arms unfolded in order to indicate as useless the approach of his theatre without illusions, an old man whom this companionship with an instrument of noise and attraction seduced perhaps to her unspecified project; then, as if, from what at once could be envisaged here as most beautiful, the enigma, clasp-closing the mundane one with a jewel, the lack of an answer at her breast sparkled! behold her engulfed, at my nonplussed clown's surprise before the public's coming to a stop, seized by the call of the drum's rum-tum-tum mumbling my unchanging and at first obscure to myself: "Everybody enter, it's only a penny, it will be returned to whoever is not satisfied with the show." The straw halo having been emptied into the gratitude joining two senile palms, I wave its colors, as a signal, from afar, and covered my head, ready to cut through the crowd standing in the secret of what the initiative of a contemporary of our evenings had known to make of this dreamless place.

Knee-high she was emerging, on a table, from a hundred heads.

Clear, as a beam strayed from somewhere flashed her forth electrically, this calculation bursts forth for me, that, for want of everything, she, according as fashion, a fantasy, or the mood of heaven enhanced her beauty, was amply paying, without the addition of dance or song, the crowd for the alms exacted in favor of someone; and in the same instant I understand my duty in the peril of the subtle exhibition, or that the one earthly resource one had, in order to ward off the defection of curiosities was to resort to some absolute power like that of Metaphor. Quickly, spout until the elucidation upon many features, of their freedom from apprehension which, not grasping everything all at once, surrenders to the evidence, even though with difficulty, implied in the word and consents to exchanging its cheap coin for exact and superior presumptions, in short, the certainty for everyone of not being cheated.

A glance, the last, at hair where smokes and then lights up with the show of gardens the paleness of the crepe hat of the same shade as the statuesque dress, rising over a foot hydrangea-colored like the rest, advancing toward the spectator.

Then:

> The hair, flight of a flame at the extreme
> Occident of desires, to unfurl it all
> Goes down (I'd say a diadem dying)
> Towards the crowned forehead, its ancient hearth
>
> But without gold sigh that this live cloud
> The ignition of the always internal fire
> Originally the only one, should continue
> In the jewel of the eye serious or laughing
>
> A nakedness of tender hero defames
> The one who moving no star or fires on her finger
> Only to simplify with glory the woman
> Accomplishes darting lightning with her head the exploit
>
> Of sowing with rubies the doubt she skins
> Like a joyous and tutelary torch.

My aiding the waist of the living allegory, which was already giving up its post, perhaps because of a failing on my part of an ulterior flow of words, in order gently to soften its downward bound: "I shall have you note," I added, now on a level with the understanding of the visitors, cutting short their astonishment before this dismissal by an affection of a return to the authenticity of the show, "Ladies and Gentlemen, that the person who has had the honor of submitting herself to your judgment does not need, to convey the sense of her charm to you, a costume nor any other customary theater accessory. This naturalness makes the best of the perfect allusion which dress always makes to one of woman's primordial incentives, and suffices, as your kindly approbation convinces me." A suspense of appreciation, except for some confounding "O sure!" or "That's it!" and "Yes" from the throats as several bravos offered by pairs of generous hands, led the crowd, with which we were going to mingle, to the exit upon an emptiness of trees and the night, were it not for the waiting, still, of a childish soldier boy in white gloves who was dreaming of unstiffening them through the assessment of a haughty garter.

"Thank you," the dear one consented, a gust of constellation or leaves come straight at her drunken as if to find in it if not the recovery of her equanimity, she had not doubted of success, at least the customary coolness of her voice: I have in mind the memory of things which are unforgettable.

"Oh, nothing but the commonplace of an aesthetic . . ."

"Which you might perhaps not have introduced, who knows? my friend, the pretext of thus formulating before me in the conjunct isolation, for example, of our carriage – where is it – let us get back to it: but it burst forth, forced out by the brutal blow in the stomach caused by the impatience of people to whom at any price and suddenly one must proclaim something, even a revery . . ."

"Which does not know itself and dashes, naked with fear, across the public; it's true. As you, Madame, would not have heard so irrefutably, despite its reduplication on a rhyme of the final stroke, my flattery according to a primitive kind of sonnet, I wager, if each term had not reverberated to you from various tympani to charm a mind open to multiple comprehension."

"Perhaps!" accepted our thought the same in a playfulness of nocturnal breezes.   ᵔᵍ

Our detailed elucidation of the sonnet comes in an appendix.[1] First the prose poem proper.

Silence begins the proceedings in a natural way. Any woman at his side, like reveries (a reservoir of quiet joy) while the carriage motion and whirring wheels lull them and calm the sudden interjection of wayside flowers – and one woman in particular knows this (his lady friend, originally Méry Laurent no doubt) – would exempt him from the effort of saying anything, in the sense that anything uttered would be, in this perfect setting, *de trop*. That will be the flattering conceit of the sonnet. There is the possible overlapping idea of such women's lack of intellectuality.[2] Any compliment on her dress – which is like a tacit question, almost an offer to the companion male (but calling for no *verbal* response) – could, by contrast with (and opposition to) all this chance assemblage (of delights and promises) only emphasize the *distance* – between the word and preciously whole, quiet beauty; by extension, between clumsy male and self-sufficient female – which would be registered in her face *via* a knowing smile.

But reality does not respect such serenity:[3] besides the expiring gleam on the landau's varnish (the "luxury" is both the sundown spectacle and the carriage's) there was, pitilessly (the fall of the perfect mood is also day's demise) a sort of stormy vociferation, all at once and without apparent cause, of the ordinary strident laughter of things [4] – everyday loud, vain, healthy, on-going reality – and the triumphant brass of vulgarity.[5] This noise was like the cacophony in the ears of anyone who, distracted for a moment by his thoughts (rather than being totally lost in them), remains alert before the insistent presence (or "haunting") of existence. You cannot get away from it, we say . . .

"The So-and-so fair" and some sort of suburban rendezvous! – announced the girl being vehicled amid distractions, her voice free of any annoyance (as contrasted with the poet's pique at the vulgar interruption); so Mallarmé obeyed the implied wish and stopped the carriage.

There is no compensation for this jolt other than a need to *figure* it artistically in such as way as to be plausible to (and calm) his mind, just as suspended lamps, lit up little by little (the fair's strings of lights coming on now, and a metaphor for this crystallizing vision) arrange themselves symmetrically in garlands and symbols. So he decides to make the most of his wrecked solitude and plunge courageously into this deliberate ("exprès": everything seems to conspire to annoy him) and hateful outburst of everything he had fled in graceful company. She is ready and shows no surprise, leaning on him (literally and figuratively) as he assists her from the carriage, and they go down the central dazzled lane of the fair dividing equally rowdy shows on each side and making a little closed-in world for a crowd – their limited perspective is fully implied.

I paraphrase the next paragraph:

Following the assaults (on their consciousness) of a mediocre libertinism – tacky sideshows – there detained us – for the sake of anything which would divert our stagnant mood[6] (which was amused, incidentally, by the growing dusk in the background, bizarre and purple) – equally with the incendiary sunset-cloud (there detained us) a poignant human spectacle: an apparently empty booth, (its emptiness) denied by the garish frame of the inscription in capital letters.

More paraphrase:

Regardless of who owned this ripped-open mattress (shoddy cloth on which the inscription was written, which was displayed in order) to improvise here, like veils in all times and temples, a mystery![7] its figuration during the fast had not aroused in its possessor, before he unrolled it as the banner of joyous hopes, the hallucination of some marvel to show (except the inanity of his hungry nightmare).

The plainer meaning is that when he slept on the former mattress cover, he had (despite his possible ascetic fasting, propitious to vision) dreamed up nothing for his show. The "hungry nightmare" is both his poverty-stricken fasting and the arid dreams plus the current nightmarish garish emptiness confronting them.

Going on:

Nevertheless, moved by the fraternal (implying the group-pull on the booth-owner) character of exception to daily misery which a meadow derives – when the mysterious word "festival" institutes it – from the many shoes trampling it (for this "ritual") there arises in the depths of clothes some singular whim of taking out the hard penny for the sole reason of spending,[8] he too! no matter who, stripped of everything except the idea here was an opportunity to be one of the chosen – if not to sell, to show, but what? – had yielded to the convocation of the benign rendezvous. Or else, very prosaically, perhaps the trained rat – unless the beggar counted on his athletic muscles to win popular fascination – was missing, at the crucial moment, as often happens when a man is put on the spot by general circumstances.

This is a modest version of the overall theme of *Un Coup de dés jamais n'abolira le hasard*, where the general "circumstances" also surround an attempted *coup* against fate.

Mallarmé presents here (in advance, as usual) something like the carnival of Bakhtin or the potlatch of Bataille: a deep need to return to Source behind the parallel expressions of *spending* and a subtly suggested sexuality; not all that subtly, actually, given the sexy and corny atmosphere at such fairs.[9] Later in the piece, the same motif is clearly attached to a soldier who dreams of "unstiffening" his gloved hand by caressing the lady's garter.

The humor of this punctilious prose, contrasted with the pitifully abject sense is keen. The image of the poor booby pulled irresistibly by fashion is, in a way, that of all mankind, as a spirit like Mallarmé's – or Dante's, Swift's, Voltaire's, Joyce's – spontaneously sees it, often.

More paraphrase:

"Beat the drum," regally proposed Madame – you (female) alone know Who – (here the piece is clearly addressed to Méry) – indicating an ancient drum from (beside) which there arose – uncrossing his arms to show it was useless to approach his unprestigious theater – an old man whom this association with an instrument of noise and attraction, perhaps, seduced to her unspecified plan; then, as if the enigma of what one might suddenly imagine here as most beautiful sparkled (revealing itself) through a jewel[10] clasping the (dress-collar on the) breast of the worldly lady like the lack of response (i.e. the enigmatic silence) on her throat, behold her swallowed up, to the surprise of the dumbfounded clown I felt myself to be, in front of a halt of the public held by the rising rum-tum-tum which muffled my invariable and, at first, obscure to myself, barking

"Step up, everybody, it's only a penny; money back to anybody who isn't satisfied with the show."

Having emptied the straw-hat halo (Mallarmé's hat in which he had collected the pennies) into two palms (of the old man) joined in thanks, I wave its colors as a signal from afar (to Méry) and put it on, ready to cut through the mass standing in the secret (i.e. unknowing: also, the mass hid her from him at first) of what the initiative of a contemporary of our evenings had been able to make of this lacklustre place.

At knee-height (the table's), she emerged, on a table, from the hundred heads.

Clear as a beam of light gone astray from somewhere which electrically stabbed her (i.e. she is spotlighted and it is like his new idea flashing) there bursts forth this calculation that, lacking everything (outside herself) She, depending on fashion, a fantasy or the mood of heaven to bring out her beauty, without dance or song, amply repaid the throng for the alms required to benefit a random being (the old man); at the same moment, I understood my duty in (amidst) the peril of the subtle exhibition, or that the only way in the world to ward off defection in the curiosities (of the public) was to resort to some absolute power like that of a metaphor. Quickly, yell out something until (I could see) the brightening, in many countenances, of their sense of security which – not seizing everything at once – yields to the evidence (even when difficult or obscure) implied in speech ("the word"), and (thus satisfied) consents to exchange its cheap coin for exact and superior ideas (which constitute something for their money), in short, the certainty for all of not being cheated.

(I gave) a last glance at the head of hair where there smokes, then lights up with the feast-for-the-eyes of gardens the paling (next to the flowers) of a crepe hat of the same tone as the statuesque dress pulled up over a foot hydrangea color like the rest and advancing toward the spectators.

Then comes the sonnet, which we treat in the appendix. Paraphrasing further:

My aid to the waist (helping her gently down) of the living allegory who was already giving up her post, perhaps because of the lack of further words on

my part, "Note," I added, now on a level with the understanding of the
visitors (his present plain speech as opposed to the obscure poetry), cutting
short their stupefaction at the leave-taking (of the lady) by a pretence of
return to the authenticity of the show, (Note) Ladies and Gentlemen, that
the person who has had the honor of submitting herself to your appreciation does not need in order to convey the sense of her charm to you, a
costume or any other usual theater accessory. This naturalness makes the
most of the perfect allusion which dress always makes to one of women's
primordial motives, and is sufficient as your kindly approval shows me."

He is referring to the age-old association of women and flowers.
They both attract for the sake of perpetuation; both spring with
pure life.

A silence of the appreciative sort, apart from some baffling "Of course" or
"That's it" and "Yes" as well as several "Bravos" supplied by generous
pairs of hands led the crowd as far as the exit, on to an emptiness of trees
and night, (the crowd) among which we were going to mingle had it not
been for the juvenile soldier boy waiting in white gloves ("still"; yet
unsullied; etc.) which he dreamed of taking the stiffness out of by
appraising (with his gloved hand) a haughty garter (the relatively upper
class lady's, also high on the leg).

"Thanks" the dear woman consented, having drunk in a gust of
constellations and leaves (in the night air) to find there if not reassurance –
for she hadn't doubted of her success – at least the habitual cool of her
voice: "I have a memory of unforgettable things."

"Oh, nothing but the commonplace of an aesthetic." (This is Mallarmé's
succinct explanation of the sonnet.)

That you could not perhaps have introduced – who knows, my (male)
friend, the pretext of formulation (i.e. what cause for the sonnet might
have arisen) in front of me in the joint isolation for example of our carriage
– where is it? – let's go back to it – but this spurted out, forced from the
brutal punch in the stomach caused by an impatience of people to whom at
any cost one must proclaim something, even a day-dream. (He adds)
Which is unaware of itself and plunges naked with fear through the public;
it's true. Just as you, Madame, wouldn't have heard so irrefutably (in spite
of its repetition in a rhyme at the end) my compliment according to a
primitive mode of the sonnet, I bet, if each term hadn't been bounced back
at you by various tympani, to claim a mind open to multiple understanding.

Again, the feminine is seen as less intellectually concentrated,
naturally. Plurality, as in *Un Spectacle interrompu* and the *Faune*,
etc., is her special realm: "'Perhaps,' the same (lady) accepted our
thought in a playfulness of nocturnal breath (breezes, airs)."

The syntactical ambiguity here allows a reading of "our thought"
as being Mallarmé's own "better half," or *anima*, as in "mon âme,

une si exquise dame anormale" (p. 293), "Psyché, mon âme," and other such references we mention in our comment on the sonnet, below.

We observed earlier the going out from self implied in the prose dimension of the prose poem generally, and that woman can fill that role as Other by becoming a *vous* as opposed to a *tu* or some equivalent distancing (this happens slightly in *Frisson d'hiver* and *La Pipe*); but here the lady is very much a *tu*, a part of the co-subjectivity, as the emphasis on silence makes clear. She moves slightly in the Other direction insofar as she is "open to multiple understanding." Mallarmé once said that "La foule délègue auprès de vous son représentant, votre femme," but that darker half-truth is subdued here, as is usual for him (as compared with, say, Baudelaire). No, the Other being explored here is clearly the crowd, which Mallarmé, with his integral understanding and generosity – as we shall see particularly in *Conflit* – saw as "including genius" (p. 383).

At least it listens to it, in this case . . . Well, he knew the odds and the improbabilities in such circumstances, but he never ceased to dream of getting his rare vision across to everybody. That is what the stubborn manoeuverings surrounding the project of *Le Livre* were mainly about.

APPENDIX
La Chevelure vol d'une flamme

This late sonnet was published for the first time as part of the prose poem *La Déclaration foraine* (in the 12 August 1887 issue of *L'Art et la Mode*).[1]

The poem is a celebration of a woman whose looks, featuring her magnificent hair, need no outer adornment. The earlier prose poem *Le Phénomène futur* was based on a similar idea (including the sideshow setting, inherited from Banville or Baudelaire): "Je t'apporte . . . une Femme d'autrefois. Quelque folie, originelle et naïve, une extase, d'or, je ne sais quoi! par elle nommeé sa chevelure," and so on (p. 269). In *La Déclaration foraine*, Mallarmé tells, with an air of fantasy, based on some unknown element of fact, how this lady friend (Méry) insisted on their stopping in at a carnival. Seeing an empty stall, Madame impulsively tells an old drummer, seated nearby, to attract a public; whereupon she climbs on a table. Mallarmé realizes that something must be done for the crowd, which has paid admission and might not appreciate, as he does, a mere look at Méry. The poem ostensibly explains to them what they are getting. Actually, the sonnet was, without doubt, written separately and was combined with the prose as an afterthought; its imagery is occasionally inconsistent with the unlikely situation. This view is supported by the fact that Mallarmé published it separately in his *Poésies* and therefore its imagery must be independent of any notion of a crowd–public.

La chevelure vol d'une flamme à l'extrême	The hair flight of a flame at the extreme
Occident de désirs pour la tout déployer	Occident of desires to unfurl it all
Se pose (je dirais mourir un diadème)	Goes down (I'd say a diadem dying)
Vers le front couronné son ancien foyer	Towards the crowned forehead its ancient hearth
Mais sans or soupirer que cette vive nue	But without [deprived of] gold sigh [imperative, addressed to himself, in the hope] that this live cloud
L'ignition du feu toujours intérieur	The ignition of the always internal fire
Originellement la seule continue	Originally the only [cloud] should continue
Dans le joyau de l'œil véridique ou rieur	In the jewel of the eye serious or laughing

The hair flares up,[2] like the pleasure of the admiring poet; the mistress is undoubtedly combing it out full length in front of her mirror, as in *Quelle soie* where it is likewise called a "cloud": "la torse et native nue / Que hors de ton miroir tu tends." It is a momentary revelation, a flash of beauty; then it dies down as she arranges it in a braid–crown about her forehead, where it had been "originally."[3] The poet sighs and hopes (or "tells himself"; Noulet) the gift of delight will continue in his sweetheart's eyes.[4] This lover's *soupirer* – compare *Soupir* – is inconsistent with Richard's notion that the eye is the crowd–public's; that would be too much of a leap, and nothing in the sonnet itself announces it.

An association with sunset is clear in the use of the term *occident*, the West (this harmony of fair hair and sunset-glories was the core of *Victorieusement fui* and, partly, *M'introduire dans ton histoire*). As in *Toast funèbre*, the sun–source of all love is implied; the one original Eros from which this beauty springs is "the internal fire / Originally the only (life-cloud)"; compare "foyer placé au centre de l'univers total" (p. 1192) or "feu . . . le vieux secret d'ardeurs et splendeurs qui s'y tord" (p. 295).

extrême occident de désirs pour la tout déployer: means that the hair is combed out to an extreme point of desire in the watching poet – "desire to unfurl it all" – where it can only fall, or set like the sun having reached the horizon, having run its course of light, as in "la chimère, en la limite de son geste, qui va redescendre" (p. 390). It has also been suggested (by Chadwick and others) that Mallarmé is referring to his declining powers (the poem dates from his forty-fifth year).

pour la tout déployer has a possible meaning of *"in spite of* its all being unfurled (it will fall)"; compare "déroulant ta tresse en flots" (p. 23). It may also imply the spreading fires of sunset (Chisholm).

mourir un diadème: reminds us of the fireworks–hair–Eros of *M'introduire*, "Comme mourir pourpre la roue," a flooding afterglow of dying pleasure, as in Baudelaire's *Jet d'eau*:

> L'éclair brûlant des voluptés
> S'élance, rapide et hardie
> Vers les vastes cieux enchantés,
> Puis, elle s'épanche, mourante
> En un flot de triste langueur.

mais sans or: Now that the hair is braided, the golden flash is gone; compare "sans flambeau" (p. 1481), the disappearance of sunset gold; or "Soleil couché . . . Or parti" (*Tombeau d'Anatole*, f.59); also "Sans or avec le soleil nous partons" (p. 185), an ambiguous idea of leaving moneyless and sunless.

cette vive nue / L'ignition du feu toujours intérieur: the visible "cloud" or flame above the head had arisen from the one inner flame of life or love (the *nue* as "naked" is discussed below). In the same way, the "ors ignorés" were the source of Hérodiade's visible light of eyes and hair: "pierres où mes yeux . . . empruntent leur clarté mélodieuse, et vous / Métaux qui donnez à ma jeune chevelure / Une splendeur"; compare "Tous les rêves émerveillés . . . ne produisent fleur sur la joue / Dans l'œil diamants impayés" (*Rondel I*).

feu: there is a slight hint of a "dead" (*feu*) flame to be
revivified: "l'arrière mais renaissante flamme" (p. 402).

intérieur: "le regard limpide et rieur / Verse ... / son
charmant être *intérieur*" (p. 124); "foyer ... les inté-
rieurs" (p. 1192); "très à l'intérieur" (*Coup de Dés*, page
3), the womb–source (*L'Œuvre de Mallarmé*, p. 150).

originellement: "Quelque folie, *originelle* et naïve, une
extase d'or je ne sais quoi! par elle nommé sa chevelure"
(p. 269).

véridique ou rieur: this is part of the "doubt" of the last line,
whether the eye mocks him or favors him with an *authentic* glimpse of the original fire: "véridiques, à même"
(p. 385).

Une nudité de héros tendre diffame	A nakedness of tender hero defames
Celle qui ne mouvant astre ni feux au doigt	The one [woman, nakedness] who waving no star or fires on her finger
Rien qu'à simplifier avec gloire la femme	Only to simplify with glory the woman
Accomplit par son chef fulgurante l'exploit	Accomplishes darting lightning with her head the exploit
De semer de rubis le doute qu'elle écorche	Of sowing with rubies the doubt she grazes [skins]
Ainsi qu'une joyeuse et tutélaire torche.	Like a joyous and tutelary torch.

The syntax is ambiguous: "A tender lover's nudity defames the
(feminine) Nudity which accomplishes – merely to simplify with
glory the woman (object) – the exploit. Or "woman" is in appo-
sition with "The one ..." and both together constitute the subject
of "accomplished."

In either case, the sense is that a lover (even tender Mallarmé) is
de trop here, can only "defame," degrade, the feast of pure beauty;
she suffices alone, as Hérodiade did. The "nakedness" of his art
yields to hers. Another gallant implication is, likely, that Mallarmé's mistress – perhaps anyone's – is defamed if anyone claims
she must sleep with a man to bring him joy; she has this other
important way. (Richard sees the *nudité* as referring to Mallarmé's
sense of exposure before the crowd. But we doubt that he had a
crowd in mind when he composed the poem. Her public is her
lover.)

héros: has the strong overtone of Eros, as usual in Mallarmé;
see under *M'introduire dans ton histoire* in *Toward the
Poems of Mallarmé*.

Celle: is ambiguous – the woman, the nakedness (the simple
unadorned woman's hair, her essence), recalling the
similar *native nue* of *Quelle soie* (*q.v.*).

celle qui ne mouvant astre ni feux au doigt: she (or it) needs
no external light, such as jewelry (variant; "Celle qui ne
mouvant bagues ni feux au doigt" (p. 1461)). Compare
"déploie avec l'émoi seul de sa robe ma très peu con-
sciente . . . inspiratrice" (p. 308). The early *Sonnet à Wyse*
had the same idea of sufficiency without trappings: "la
chevelure nue / Que loin des bijoux tu défends"; "son
doigt tremblait, sans améthyste / Et nu" (p. 22); "sans
flambeau" (*Victorieusement fui*).[5]

diffame: "on a diffamé l'Art" (p. 569).

simplifier: "simplification apportée par un regard de
voyant" (p. 696); "la *nudité* d'une âme *simplifiée* . . .
redevenir primitif" (*Propos sur la poésie*, p. 159); recall
the *nue* above. The idea of a back-to-the-source flash is
found in a crudely erotic context in "dégorger cet éclair,
vers quelque reddition de comptes *simplificatrice*"
(p. 322). A usage closer to the present one, the idea of a
superbly direct and "naked" beauty – "la chevelure nue"
– combined with conscious art is implied in "elle [la
danseuse] te livre à travers le voile dernier, qui toujours
reste, la *nudité* de tes *concepts*" (p. 307); or "jet délicat et
vierge et une jumelle clairvoyance directe du *simple*; qui,
peut-être, avaient à s'accorder encore" (p. 298). The
notion, expressed in all these excerpts, of an unconscious,
spontaneous, feminine collaborator with his aesthetic is
found in the prose poem where the sonnet was imbedded
and recited. There, Mallarmé refers to his own poem as a
"lieu commun d'une esthétique," and the idea of a
stripped *base* for his art runs through the prose as well as
the little poem: "la personne qui a eu l'honneur de se
soumettre à votre jugement ne requiert pour vous communiquer le sens de son charme, un costume ou aucun
accessoire usuel du théâtre . . . Ce *naturel* s'accommode
de l'allusion parfaite que fournit la toilette [flowers in her
hat] toujours à l'un des motifs primordiaux de la femme"
(p. 282). This concept of an art that is a synthesis of nature

and form is developed more explicitly in "Bucolique" (p. 402):

"Le double adjuvant aux lettres, extériorité et moyen ont, envers un, dans l'ordre absolu, gradué leur influence" and "La première en date, la nature. Idée tangible pour intimer quelque réalité aux sens frustes et, compensation, *directe* . . . au *foyer* subtil (de la musique) je reconnus, sans douter, l'*arrière* [cf. *feu* . . . *intérieur*] mais *renaissante flamme*, où se sacrifièrent les bosquets et les cieux."

That is, the natural sunset is prolonged in the tamed flame of aesthetic joy. In the same passage is found the corollary idea of a distillation (whereby the corruption of the artificial is purified in sacrificial flame), the "ardent, volatile dépouillement en traits."[6] In sum, the *tresse(s)* of the *maîtresse*, as original source and distilled verbal *traits*, will do for poetry.

semer: the "sparks" of light are like the "sown" constellation (*L'Œuvre de Mallarmé*, p. 418) of the *Coup de Dés* versus the dark night of chance or "doubt"; compare "mon doute amas de nuit ancienne" (*Faune*: note the dark *ou*); in the *Sonnet à Wyse* this was expressed as "étincelles d'Etre."[7]

doute qu'elle écorche: the light not only touches but *cuts into the substance of* the darkness, a visual effect of sparkling, the light mingling with the dark: "renaissante flamme . . . le manque du rêve [doubt] qu'elle consume" (p. 402); "fulguration . . . consumait l'ombre" (p. 395); "L'Espérance rebrousse . . . la Nuit noire" (p. 23). A possible hint of English "scorch" has been noted by others.

rubis: the simple flame sows rubies, as the pure authentic burning of the poet gives off these refined "stars," the "ardent, volatile dépouillement en traits qui se correspondent, maintenant proches la pensée" (p. 402); compare the burning cigar of art in *Toute l'âme résumée*. The image of hair jewels is prominent in the *Faune, M'introduire*, and to some extent in Baudelaire's *La Chevelure*.

doute: if we accept a link with the prose (even as an afterthought), the doubt could be that of the "crowd," for example, that one described in the prose poem: her hair is a "luminous evidence," like the *astre en fête* of *Quand l'ombre* or the flame of Baudelaire's "tutelary" art in the *Tombeau*, twisted as it was by the winds of public mocking and scepticism; or the poet's flame in *Tout orgueil*, which is also a *torche*, not only "grazed" but extinguished by the wind of disbelief. Yet, as in the case of Baudelaire or of Villiers, the confrontation with the crowd (*cf.* "Confrontation") was necessary to literary production: "ceci jaillit, forcé, sous le coup de poing brutal à l'estomac, que cause une impatience de gens" (p. 283). In this sense, the crowd is subtly compared to the merely human aspect of the lady friend who insists on outer results: "Comme vous Madame" (p. 283); compare "La Dame, Notre Patronne . . . la foule" (p. 383); "la foule, délègue . . . quelqu'un qui la représente: sa femme" (*Documents iconographiques*, p. 42).

A more important sense of *doute*, independent of the prose, is the overall metaphysical misgiving about Beauty or Truth – "le doute du Jeu suprême" (*Une dentelle*) – which is now, once again, miraculously abolished: "irrésistiblement au foyer subtil, je reconnus, *sans douter*, l'arrière mais renaissante flamme" (p. 402). It is the old Phoenix of his artistic faith, as in *Ses purs ongles*.

The doubt is also, secondarily, that of Mallarmé's personal relationship; he wondered, in the quatrains, whether she was serious or mocked him – but the flame of love quells that uneasiness.

The *vive nue* is, in part, that natural or "live" nudity, or nude woman.

écorche: in the sense of "skins" this word may evoke an image of blood from the *rubis*.

Austin Gill has proposed a radically different interpretation, which runs as follows: the hair is a flame stolen (*vol*, in that sense) from the original Eros-flame – either by the poet, who displays it in his sonnet (or before the crowd in the prose poem) or by the lady who wears it – that eternal *voleuse* as Mallarmé called her in the Huret interview, for wearing a beauty properly the poet's; and the rest of the poem says that it is a defamation of poetry – "Celle . . . qui accomplit par son chef" – to wish (*soupirer*) that antique amours (*nudité de héros tendre*) be continued (*continue*) in modern guise through a contemporary lady; no, that is over, poetry itself suffices. Thus the *front couronné* is the Banvillean idea of the poet crowned with laurel (Mallarmé did indeed celebrate this image in his "Symphonie littéraire"). The *occident* would be the modern decadence of the West when all this restitution is happening, as in *Le Phénomène futur*.

81

This interpretation makes for many difficulties when presented as *the* meaning: despite Gill, the hair is obviously still the core of the poem, persisting through the "la femme / Accomplit par son chef fulgurante l'exploit." The *se pose* refers easily to an idea of flight alighting or going down, less readily to Gill's notion that it means it "abdicates" in favor of a poet. The change from female hair to male brow is too abrupt and unpoetic, not at all typical of Mallarmé. It is far likelier that he had in mind here a subtle metamorphosis like the one from muse–hair to art in the *Tombeau de Charles Baudelaire*. Finally, the tone of the whole is violated by this exclusive slant: the celebration of woman (her hair) as a rival of art but also the unconscious source which it draws from is central to Mallarmé, as in *Victorieusement fui*, the early *Château de l'espérance, Quelle soie aux baumes de temps, De l'orient passé des Temps*, and the *Tombeau de Charles Baudelaire* as well as the prose poems *Le Phénomène futur* and *La Déclaration foraine*.

But if we accept Gill's version as a counterpointed theme, it does help to explain some puzzling things: the *pour* in particular and the complex syntax in general. I must confess that I feel Mallarmé went too far in this poem.

10

LE NÉNUPHAR BLANC

Monet was an admiring friend. When you go to Giverny, almost the first thing you see in the house is a photo portrait of Mallarmé facing the entrance. We cannot help feeling the mood of late nineteenth-century, late Romantic, impressionist–symbolist, exquisite refinement, the stippled fluviality of French expression fraternally in Monet when we read this subtle prose crystallizing the image of a water lily. It is equally present in the musical impressionism of Debussy and Ravel – *Reflets dans l'eau*, *Sonatine*, *Jardins sous la pluie* – "festivals of light," water, air, foliage, splashes of sensual whiteness floating magically free in art of diamantine precision, a *Jeu suprême*...

In Monet, notoriously, one hardly knows where sky melts iridescently into reflecting water, any more than in Proust's version of him, Elstir, one knew where land was, where sea. In Mallarmé's prose poem, one is hard put to decide what is pungently plunging sexuality and what is ethereal transcendence. That is, of course, the nature of the metaphoric dimension, that undecidability between extremes which trace a circular course until, somewhere, they meet. The finest lyric art – Shakespeare's, Keats's, Rimbaud's, Moussorgsky's – at its deepest heals our torn Dionysian psyches in this embracing way.

The central image is the white water lily, which is the emblem of the virtual lady hidden in her garden, whom Mallarmé *almost* encounters; but he chooses to preserve intact the excruciating presence–absence[1] so typical of his aesthetic.[2] The absence and the presence have close cognates in the flawless ideal and its maddening erotic opposite,[3] just as the rose does in the *Romaunt de la rose*.[4]

The sensuality can scarcely be denied in phrases like "je m'immisce à de sa confuse intimité" or the image of the shadow in the inviolate girdle with its diamond clasp.[5] But just how this relates to Mallarmé's total poetic vision is too complex for intercalation in a brief introduction here. Having worked it out in connection with the *Coup de Dés*, I present it in its integrality in an appendix to this chapter. Briefly, however, the *creuse blancheur* is a woman's womb emptiness, source of original creation, *ex nihilo*, and also the male equivalent; this vibrant notion is the core of various seminal poems, notably *Une dentelle s'abolit*, where the hollow mandolin is just such an inviolate, pure source of possible art of the sort Mallarmé sadly, melodiously dreamed of.

ತ∽

Le Nénuphar blanc

J'avais beaucoup ramé, d'un grand geste net assoupi, les yeux au-dedans fixés sur l'entier oubli d'aller, comme le rire de l'heure coulait alentour. Tant d'immobilité paressait que frôlé d'un bruit inerte où fila jusqu'à moitié la yole, je ne vérifiai l'arrêt qu'à l'étincellement stable d'initiales sur les avirons mis à nu, ce qui me rappela à mon identité mondaine.

Qu'arrivait-il, où étais-je?

Il fallut, pour voir clair en l'aventure, me remémorer mon départ tôt, ce juillet de flamme, sur l'intervalle vif entre ses végétations dormantes d'un toujours étroit et distrait ruisseau, en quête des floraisons d'eau et avec un dessein de reconnaître l'emplacement occupé par la propriété de l'amie d'une amie, à qui je devais improviser un bonjour. Sans que le ruban d'aucune herbe me retînt devant un paysage plus que l'autre chassé avec son reflet en l'onde par le même impartial coup de rame, je venais échouer dans quelque touffe de roseaux, terme mystérieux de ma course, au milieu de la rivière: où tout de suite élargie en fluvial bosquet, elle étale un nonchaloir d'étang plissé des hésitations à partir qu'a une source.

L'inspection détaillée m'apprit que cet obstacle de verdure en pointe sur la courant, masquait l'arche unique d'un pont prolongé, à terre, d'ici et de là, par une haie clôturant des pelouses. Je me rendis compte. Simplement le parc de Madame . . . , l'inconnue à saluer.

Un joli voisinage, pendant la saison, la nature d'une personne qui s'est choisi retraite aussi humidement impénétrable ne pouvant être que conforme à mon goût. Sûr, elle avait fait de ce cristal son miroir intérieur à l'abri de l'indiscrétion éclatante des après-midi; elle y venait et la buée d'argent glaçant des saules ne fut bientôt que la limpidité de son regard habitué à chaque feuille.

Toute je l'évoquais lustrale.

Courbé dans la sportive attitude où me maintenait de la curiosité, comme sous le silence spacieux de ce que s'annonçait l'étrangère au commencement d'esclavage dégagé par une possibilité féminine: que ne signifiaient pas mal les courroies attachant le soulier de rameur au bois de l'embarcation, comme on ne fait qu'un avec l'instrument de ses sortilèges.

" – Aussi bien une quelconque … " allais-je terminer

Quand un imperceptible bruit me fit douter si l'habitante du bord hantait mon loisir, ou inespérément le bassin.

Le pas cessa, pourquoi?

Subtil secret des pieds qui vont, viennent, conduisent l'esprit où le veut la chère ombre enfouie en de la batiste et les dentelles d'une jupe affluant sur le sol comme pour circonvenir du talon à l'orteil, dans une flottaison, cette initiative par quoi la marche s'ouvre, tout au bas et les plis rejetés en traîne, une échappée, de sa double flèche savante.

Connaît-elle un motif à sa station, elle-même la promeneuse: et n'est-ce, moi, tendre trop haut la tête, pour ces joncs à ne dépasser et toute la mentale somnolence où se voile ma lucidité, que d'interroger jusque-là le mystère.

" – A quel type s'ajustent vos traits, je sens leur précision, Madame, interrompre chose installée ici par le bruissement d'une venue, oui! ce charme instinctif d'en dessous que ne défend pas contre l'explorateur la plus authentiquement nouée, avec une boucle en diamant, des ceintures. Si vague concept se suffit: et ne transgressera le délice empreint de généralité qui permet et ordonne d'exclure tous visages, au point que la révélation d'un (n'allez point le pencher, avéré, sur le furtif seuil où je règne) chasserait mon trouble, avec lequel il n'a que faire. "

Ma présentation, en cette tenue de maraudeur aquatique, je la peux tenter, avec l'excuse du hasard.

Séparés, on est ensemble: je m'immisce à de sa confuse intimité, dans ce suspens sur l'eau où mon songe attarde l'indécise, mieux que visite, suivie d'autres, l'autorisera. Que de discours oiseux en comparaison de celui que je tins pour n'être pas entendu, faudra-t-il, avant de retrouver aussi intuitif accord que maintenant, l'ouïe au ras de l'acajou vers le sable entier qui s'est tu!

La pause se mesure au temps de ma détermination.

Conseille, ô mon rêve, que faire?

Résumer d'un regard la vierge absence éparse en cette solitude et, comme on cueille, en mémoire d'un site, l'un de ces magiques nénuphars clos qui y surgissent tout à coup, enveloppant de leur creuse blancheur un rien, fait de songes intacts, du bonheur qui n'aura pas lieu et de mon souffle ici retenu dans la peur d'une apparition, partir avec; tacitement, en déramant peu à peu sans du heurt briser l'illusion ni que le clapotis de la bulle visible d'écume enroulée à ma fuite ne jette aux pieds survenus de la personne la ressemblance transparente du rapt de mon idéale fleur.

Si, attirée par un sentiment d'insolite, elle a paru, la Méditative ou la Hautaine, la Farouche, la Gaie, tant pis pour cette indicible mine que j'ignore à jamais! car j'accomplis selon les règles la manœuvre: me dégageai, virai et je contournais déjà une ondulation du ruisseau, emportant comme un noble œuf de cygne, tel que n'en jaillira le vol, mon imaginaire trophée, qui ne se gonfle d'autre chose sinon de la vacance exquise de soi qu'aime, l'été, à poursuivre, dans les allées de son parc, toute dame, arrêtée parfois et longtemps, comme au bord d'une source à franchir ou de quelque pièce d'eau.   ◅৪

The White Water Lily

I had rowed a lot, with a sweeping, drowsy motion my eyes turned inward fixed on the entire forgetfulness of going, as the hour's laughter flowed round about. So much motionlessness idled away the time that, brushed by a dull sound into which the skiff slipped halfway, I only verified the stop by the steady glittering of initials on the bared oars, which recalled my worldly identity to me.

What was happening, where was I?

To understand the adventure, I had to recall my early departure, in this flaming July, on the bright interval between its sleeping vegetation of a persistently narrow and rambling stream, in quest of water flowers and with the intention of exploring the site occupied by the property of a lady friend's lady friend, to whom I was to improvise a "Good day." Without any strip of grass detaining me before one landscape more than another chased away with its reflection in the water by the same impartial oar stroke, I had just run aground in some clump of reeds, mysterious end of my cruise, in the middle of a stream: where all at once the stream, widened into a fluvial grove, displays the apathy of a pond dimpled by a well-spring's hesitations to depart.

A detailed inspection revealed to me that this tapering obstacle of greenery in the current masked the single arch of a bridge prolonged, on land, on either side, by a hedge enclosing lawns. I realized. Merely the park of Madame . . . , the unknown lady I was to greet.

A pretty neighborhood, during the season; the nature of a person who has chosen herself a retreat so humidly impenetrable could only be in harmony with my taste. Surely, she had made of this crystal her interior mirror sheltered from the brilliant indiscretion of the afternoons; she would come there and the cool silvery vapor of the willows was soon only the limpidity of her glance accustomed to each leaf.

I evoked her entirely lustral.

Leaning forward in the sportive attitude in which curiosity held me, as if beneath the spacious silence with which the strange lady would announce herself, I smiled at the beginning of the servitude emanating from a feminine possibility: which the straps attaching the rower's shoes to the wood of the boat symbolized quite well, as a person is but one with the instrument of his enchantments.

"As well any woman whosoever . . . " I was going to terminate.

When an imperceptible noise made me doubt whether the inhabitant of the shore was haunting my leisure, or, contrary to all hope, the pond.

The step ceased, why?

Subtle secret of feet that go, come, lead the mind where wills, the dear shadow, buried in batiste and the lace of a skirt flowing on the ground as if to surround, from heel to toe, floatingly, this initiative by which walking opens up, very low with the folds thrown back in a train, a space with its knowing double arrow.

Does she know a reason for her standing still, the promenader herself; and would I not be holding my head too high if I raised it in order to see over these reeds and over all that mental drowsiness in which my lucidity is veiled, to interrogate so far as that the mystery?

" – To whatever type your features may adjust themselves, I feel their precision, Madame, interrupt something installed here by the rustling of an [my] arrival, yes! this instinctive charm of something beneath, which the most authentically tied of sashes, with a buckle of diamonds, does not defend against the explorer. So vague a concept suffices: and will not transgress the delight colored by generality, which permits and demands the exclusion of all faces, to the point where the revelation of one (do not bend it, verified, over the furtive threshold where I reign) would chase away my aroused emotions, with which it has no business."

My self-presentation, in this pirate's outfit, I can attempt it with the excuse of chance.

Separated, one is together: I permeate her obscure intimacy, in this suspense on the water where my dream delays the undecided one, better than any visit, followed by others, will allow it. How many trifling conversations, in comparison with the one which I made in order not to be heard, will be necessary before so intuitive an accord as now can be found again, my ear at the level of the mahogany toward the entire sand which has become silent!

The pause is measured by the time of my determination.

Advise, o my dream, what to do?

Sum up in a glance the virgin absence scattered in this solitude and, as one picks, in memory of a site, one of those magical closed water lilies which suddenly rise up there, enveloping with their hollow whiteness a nothing, made of untouched dreams, of the happiness that will not take place and of my breath held here in the fear of an apparition, leave with it; silently, rowing away little by little without breaking the illusion by a shock, and so that the splashing of the visible bubble of foam coiled up in my flight does not throw the transparent resemblance of the abduction of my ideal flower at the feet of someone coming later.

If, attracted by the feeling of something unusual, she appeared, the Meditative one or the Haughty one, the Wild one, the Gay one, too bad for that indescribable face forever unknown to me! for I accomplished the manoeuver according to the rules: disengaged myself, turned, and was already passing around an undulation of the stream, carrying away, like a noble swan's egg, such that flight will never burst forth from it, my imaginary trophy, swollen with nothing except the exquisite emptiness of self which every lady, in the summer, loves to pursue, along the walks of her park, delayed sometimes and for a long time, as if on the edge of a spring to cross or some body of water.

Mallarmé, on summer days, sailed his little sail boat, his "yole à jamais littéraire" (Valéry) on the Seine fronting his villa at Valvins, a short distance from the Château de Fontainebleau. This time he is rowing, on a narrow winding stretch, a "ruisseau"; his mind is gently lulled by the rhythmic effort and the agreeable flow of natural life, when an "inert noise brushes"[6] the hull indicating that he has been stopped and gone aground in rushes. The oars are forced out of the water, and he sees his initials (probably painted) on them, bringing the fact of his arrestation and his usual real existence back to his dreamily distracted attention.

Being thus "awakened," he recalls his having set out, this sunny July day of the world, on the "intervalle vif"[7] between dark foliage of the constricted and meandering stream, looking for water plants and also, vaguely, for the location of the estate of "l'amie d'une amie," with the thought of casually meeting her, as he had promised. No plot of grass – her estate – has detained him so far: landscape replaced landscape, reflected in the water, as he rowed on with "impartial"[8] strokes until blocked by reeds in the middle of the river where it broadens and calms into a sort of pond, surrounded by trees, with mild ripples like those of a welling spring beginning to flow. He became aware that behind the tuft of reeds forming an island's point in the middle of the stream stood a bridge leading to a bank, where to right and left extended a hedge enclosing lawns: the park of the unknown lady.[9]

She, the "inconnue" and her "parc, conforme à mon goût," are clearly related. It, the "nature d'une personne qui s'est choisi retraite aussi humidement impénétrable," is richly ambiguous: "nature" is both her nature and objective nature, just as the "miroir intérieur" is both water and feminine soul;[10] "intérieur" suggests that her mirror is a pond externally hidden in her hedged and tree-shaded property, and is also within her personal being. The universal analogy which links her fluid mirror to woman's essence is a major theme in *Hérodiade*, *Ses purs ongles*, *Frisson d'hiver* . . .

Similarly, the "buée d'argent glaçant les saules ne fut bientôt que la limpidité de son regard habitué à chaque feuille," i.e. her psychic limpidity and the objective mist "icing" the trees melt into each other with the fluency and interpenetration of much else in this impressionist atmosphere.

Toute je l'évoquais lustrale: he pictures her entirely, naturally, in the "lustral" image of her watery setting, pure and shining.

Bending over in his boat, in the posture of a rower but held there now as if under the weight of a spacious spell of silence in which he was in abeyance, he smiled at the gallantry and dependency – "esclavage" – which would ensue if the woman appeared (shades of courtly love in the style of the *Romaunt* but really of any age); this was symbolized rather well by the straps attaching his feet to the bottom boards of the boat. He ruminates further that this indicates that we are continuous with the "instrument of our attachments" (like a musician with his violin, one supposes; there is a certain analogy between the shell of the hull and a hollow instrument of art or imaginary magic, perhaps).

"*Aussi bien une quelconque . . . allais-je terminer*" implies that any woman would have that enslaving effect and offsets the divinization suggested in the preceding "lustrale." A fragment of *Les Noces d'Hérodiade* concerning "le premier venu," a passing stranger, sounds a similar note of disabused wisdom.

An "imperceptible noise" is an oxymoron, joining opposites paradoxically; what is implied is a noise so subtle as to cause unsureness as to whether it existed. That is in the mood of the whole piece, the marginal, limit-case, asymptotic elusiveness of presence–absence and the like. The doubtful sound is, obviously, in his expectant mind, that of a gentle step. But the step – if it is one – ceases, inexplicably. He imagines, born from the phantom, a female presence walking, and the whole is fraught with an exquisite erotically feminine essence, which is detailed in the appendix below. Briefly, the *ombre*, as with the disappearing nymphs of the *Faune*, represents her "secrets"; more specifically, the erotic early poem *Mystacis umbraculis* is a celebration of the female organ metaphorized as a nest, with a red bird suggesting the clitoris (compare the diamond clasp of her inviolate girdle here). The doubleness of the feet and the opening of the walk and of the train sends us to a feminine symbol frequent in Mallarmé's work, which we treat in the appendix, referring to "l'un et l'autre bord" of the boat–womb in the *Coup de Dés*, "un sein puis l'autre" in the *Noces d'Hérodiade* (her dance), the two nymphs and the "mal d'être deux" of the *Faune*, the two troupes of women adjoining the hero in *Le Livre*, the two curtains of the nuptial window–womb in *Une dentelle s'abolit* and of Hérodiade's bed, the letter *w* in *Les Mots anglais*, and so on.

The element *con* in "conduisent, concevoir, connaît-elle, contre l'explorateur, concept" and especially "je m'immisce à de sa confuse intimité" is highly suggestive.

Connaît-elle un motif à sa station indicates an uncertain, perhaps half-interested, curiosity on her part – undercurrents of her "nature."

The (*moi*) *Tendre trop haut la tête* is a male counterpart of that spontaneous interest; compare the too-tall phallic head of the little minstrel in *Pauvre Enfant pâle*, inviting a sort of cephalic cast-ration, as St Jean did. In *tendre* – to stretch forth – there is a possible overtone of "héros tendre" (*cf.* p. 78 above; also *M'introduire dans ton histoire*), reminding us vaguely of *La Carte du tendre* and its parallel with the *Romaunt de la rose*. In this passage he intimates that to interrogate the mystery (of her possible presence) by raising his head beyond the reeds which are "not to be surpassed" – in height or horizontally: they are a sort of sacred barrier protecting her privacy (compare the *sûr châtiment* following the imagined assault on Venus in the *Faune*) – would be *too much*. That *trop* is the expression of excessive vision in *Prose* (*pour des Esseintes*) and on page 7 of the *Coup de Dés*. The "mentale somnolence où se voile ma lucidité" is a sort of "leave well enough alone"; his solitary drowsy summer well-being rather resembles the solitary faun's before the advent of the divine nymphs.

If her vaguely imagined face became precise by revelation it would interrupt the magic purity of virtual vision set up by the "bruissement d'une venue" (hers). The "charme instinctif d'en dessous" is her unsullied (in the sense of unspecified) feminine essence which he, the "explorer," has discovered; it cannot be defended even by a sort of chastity belt, "la plus authentiquement nouée, avec une boucle en diamant, des ceintures." In *La Dernière Mode* Mallarmé sees himself as taking this ideal and irresistible intimate possession of his female readers: "la dame ... ressent ... jusqu'à l'âme [le livre]" (p. 500); "leur plaire ... je ne sais pas d'ambition, changée en triomphe si l'on réussit, qui aille mieux à un ouvrage" (p. 716). *M'introduire dans ton histoire* is another vaunting of this high–low conquest.

In the *Faune* there is another such imaginary penetration of a "ceinture," again with the feminine *ombre* underneath:

> ... je vais parler longtemps
> Des déesses; et par d'idolâtres peintures
> A leur ombre enlever encore des ceintures...

Jean-Pierre Richard confirms all this about the shadow: "l'espace troublant d'une ombre, d'un secret ... l'image la plus sexuelle de l'accueil" (p. 104).

The diamond (clasp), recalling the one in *La Déclaration foraine*, is found elsewhere in Mallarmé with clear erotic intent, as in the sonnet to Méry, *Dame sans trop d'ardeur*: "Pour ouïr dans la chair pleurer le diamant." Hérodiade's melting jewels, at the end of the *Scène*, are just as ambiguously but intimately sensual.

Si vague concept se suffit: the pure vision is sufficient. He asks the unknown (in a rich sense) lady not to bend her real face over the reeds and so spoil that perfection.

Then he considers that he could present himself in his water-marauder's costume (even though it is not socially formal enough), excused by the chance of the encounter. But he adds that even so, separated, they are together in a superior way virtually. And the plungingly sensuous undertone is unmistakable in "je m'immisce à de sa confuse intimité."

The suspense delays the hesitant lady, grips her, better than any concrete visit (followed in time by others, no doubt) would allow.

Suspens is a favorite word of Mallarmé's, applied to crucial images such as his version of Hamlet ("le suspens d'un acte inachevé") or the ideal representation in a theater's chandelier; it betokens an extreme union of opposites which produce, in a "lightning moment," a surpassing vision of hidden reality, as did T. S. Eliot's moment "Between two waves of the sea" (*Four Quartets*).

Many social conversations, contrasted with the unspoken one, will have to occur before such an intuitive accord can be found again; meanwhile, his ear bent over toward his mahogany boat is "conversing" only with silence, that of the sand beneath the boat, the "entier" bottom of the source. The *s'est tu* is like that of *A la nue accablante tu*, the indifferent nature beneath a shipwreck, a merely human occurrence (though here the disaster was a mild going aground).

But Mallarmé still hesitates, like Hamlet, in "suspens." The pause lasts as long as he needs to make up his mind. He consults his dream – his inner, authentic self – as to what to do. Finally, he opts for the summing-up perfection of absence, losing all, at one level, to gain all the preserved beauty of the solitary virgin place, as one plucks a magical water lily containing nothing, like the hollow mandolin belly which is the womb of ideal harmony in *Une dentelle s'abolit* or "Sous le visage en tant qu'une harmonie est pure" (*La Musique et les Lettres*). The theme is ubiquitous in Mallarmé.

The *y* and *u*[11] of "nénuphars, y, surgissent, creuse, blancheur, tout à coup"[12] are effective, along with many other *u*'s. We recall the long series of *u*'s in "boutique d'un luthier vendeur de vieux instruments pendus au mur" in *Le Démon de l'Analogie*, associated with the hollow belly of the musical instrument.

The "rien" and "n'aura pas lieu" reminds us of the "rien n'aura eu lieu" at the end of the *Coup de Dés*: a pure site like this one ("en mémoire d'un site"), but blown up to cosmic and apocalyptic proportions – without human interruption.

So he sneaks off, careful not to jar the "illusion" or to let the splash of water from his departure – with its foamy bubble, rising at the feet of "someone" arriving at the shore a bit later – betray him by bringing them a transparent (watery and/or clear) image of his theft of the ideal flower. The "resemblance" is partly that between his own bubble of illusion and the (transparent but) physical one, the actual bubble of foam. And perhaps the "clapotis" of the pricked bubble indicates in its little violence a resemblance with a *rapt* or *viol*. A further subtle analogy is between the white foam and the flower, in the well-known whiteness-chain we spoke of under

Réminiscence, which goes from the most sensual to the cloudy, just as in Hesiod Venus is born from the foam–sperm of Zeus.[13]

Mallarmé's "idéale fleur" is close to the famous one in "Je dis: une fleur! . . . musicalement se lève, idée même et suave, l'absente de tous bouquets." But the ideal in Mallarmé, as in Plato's *Symposium*, is as rooted as it is sublime; it is on the paradoxical metaphoric dimension, up and down. In music – "musicalement" – the deep sensuality *and* transcendence are typically felt; "suave" underlines that complexity.

He rehearses, once more, possible *mines* for the lady – Meditative, Haughty, Shy, Gay – and, of course, these are not allegorical, they are *real* human possibilities. No connection with the *Romaunt* here; just a raising, through capitals, to generality. That is enough to dampen the thought. Mallarmé's comments on the classical theater confirms this insight: "une époque retenue d'inventer malgré sa nature prête, dissertatrice et neutre, à vivifier le type abstrait" (pp. 319–20).

The poet, with classical navigation – *selon les règles* – withdraws, comparing his virtual flower-vision to an unhatched swan's egg, roundly perfect, like the pre-pricked bubble. We are reminded of the unflown swan of his "divine" sonnet, checked by his dream of purity, held in a sort of love–death swan-song tension or suspense, and the "absurd" of Mallarmé's overarching equivalent concept, "la fiction," vibrant and paradoxical as existence, short of the ultimate glimpse of Eden, but in its sheer ambivalence offering our closest approach to It: "costing not less than everything."

The emptiness is now seen as "vacation," "vacance de soi," that disinterested wholeness he saw in stars or *bibelots*: "où qu'ils expirent en le charme et leur désuétude . . . les bibelots abolis, sans usage" (p. 499), compared to the constellation at the end of the *Coup de Dés*, "froide de désuétude" (*cf. Ses purs ongles*).

The divinely starry essence in the purity of nothingness is expressed in some major Mallarméan texts, for example:

"Rien cette écume, vierge vers" (*Salut*)

"Musicienne du silence" (*Sainte*)

"Sylphe de ce froid profond" (*Surgi de la croupe*)

"Le Rien qui est la vérité" (*Correspondance*, Vol. 1, p. 208)

"pièce principale ou rien" (*La Musique et les Lettres*)

He imagines the lady pursuing this ideal – an ideal which is sensual, like the *Faune*, earthly, artistically full, steeped in nature – just as he had; their two visions coalesce in a sort of airy love-feast or mating, having "bu . . . à la même chimère" (*Surgi*).

She stops for a long while at the edge of a spring or some other body of water, at the brink of this transparency which we have seen resembles the hollow nenuphar: it is another symbol for pure vision or dream (water as psyche, a classical paradigm).

The swan floats on it as does the water lily or the foam related to them in the whiteness-chain together with milk. It is the liquid Source, and in this life it is to be approached only. The "cristal" or "miroir intérieur" as he calls it earlier is in a network of associations with all sorts of crystallized or frozen images – in windows, mirrors, ice-blocks, and all uncrossable – in many a crystalline text.[14]

APPENDIX

A translated extract from *L'Œuvre de Mallarmé*: *Un Coup de Dés*, slightly modified

The element *con* is very important in the *Coup de Dés*; it is a common prefix, signifying "with" in French and in other Western languages and suggesting, secondarily, another common use of the word. The circularity of its vowel *o* confirms the general tone of *con* which Mallarmé uses very often to describe Woman, or that which is feminine in a general epistemological sense; for example "Avec sa *contraire* [double] précaution, la Mère qui nous pense et nous *conçoit*" ("Catholicisme," p. 391).[1] This quotation closely comments upon the use of *con* in *circonstances*; here, too, the word signifies womb, receptacle or site for creation. The most striking example is found in *Le Nénuphar blanc* with its exquisite suggestive musicality. Here the element (and related forms) is found at least ten times in connection with "l'*inconnue* à saluer": "ce charme instinctif ... qui ne se défend pas *contre* l'explorateur la plus authentiquement nouée, avec une boucle en diamant, des ceintures. Si vague *concept* se suffit ... je m'immisce à de sa *confuse* intimité," and so on (p. 285). Here the ideal image, inviolate, finds its counterpart in the image most typical of the erotic reveries of men. It is with this image also that the poet leaves the place "en mémoire d'un *site*, l'un de ces magiques nénuphars clos qui y surgissent tout à coup, enveloppant de leur creuse blancheur un rien" (p. 286).[2] Since for Mallarmé the passive crowd is a woman, a site for the hero–poet, the following passages are discovered: "ce que de latent *contient* et d'à jamais *abscons* la présence d'une foule"

(p. 507), or "quelque chose d'occulte au fond de tous . . . quelque chose d'*abscons* . . . cette masse . . . [plusieurs individus] agissent peu délicatement, en précipitant à pareil accès la Foule . . . exposant notre Dame et Patronne à montrer sa déhiscence ou sa *lacune*" (p. 383).

The combination of duality and circularity in the two lines that describe the womb–source (page 2) is an important scheme which is renewed on page 3 and which we will return to in detail, below; let us note merely that in *Le Nénuphar blanc* we find:

Subtil secret des pieds qui vont, viennent, conduisent l'esprit où le veut la chère ombre [*cf. Mystacis umbraculis*] enfouie en de la batiste et les dentelles d'une jupe affluant sur le sol comme pour circonvenir du talon à l'orteil, dans une flottaison, cette initiative par quoi la marche s'ouvre, tout au bas et les plis rejetés en traîne, une échappée,[3] de sa double flèche savante. (p. 285)

This closely recalls a strophe of Baudelaire's *Beau navire*:

> Tes nobles jambes sous les volants qu'elles chassent,
> Tourmentent les désirs obscurs et les agacent
> Comme deux sorcières qui font
> Tourner un philtre noir dans un vase profond.

These texts are to be compared with "Virginité . . . elle-même s'est comme divisée en ses fragments de candeur, l'un et l'autre, preuves nuptiales de l'Idée" (p. 387). The "l'un et l'autre" is a Mallarméan formula for the feminine principle (duality) which is found in many of his works (see *Tryptique*, note 7, in *Toward the Poems of Mallarmé*).

The principal meaning of *l'ombre enfouie dans la profondeur par cette voile alternative* has been sketched out in our introduction to the page, where we also noted the secondary sense (a concrete one) of a wave–trough as a container of shadow, *ombre enfouie*, like the "en un puits . . . " of *Igitur* (p. 437), or Hugo's "bouche d'ombre." We noted the combination of duality (*alternative*) and circularity, whose evident concretion is the feminine organ (or womb) which is specifically developed here as an application of eternal metaphysical law. Thus in the following passage, to which we referred previously, Mallarmé associates these two feminine attributes, duality and circularity, with a third, the one we have just indicated, *l'ombre* [*enfouie*): "*ombre* enfouie en . . . jupe . . . *circonvenir* . . . *double* flèche savante" (*Le Nénuphar blanc*).

The "shadow" of *Mystacis umbraculis* (p. 22) refers unequivocally to these "feminine secrets." A subtler reference is the "Solennités tout *intimes*, l'une: de placer le couteau d'ivoire dans l'*ombre* que font *deux* pages jointes d'un volume" (p. 718). But there can be no doubt of the undertones when we juxtapose this with "Le reploiement *vierge* du livre, encore, prête à un sacrifice dont saigna la tranche rouge des anciens tomes; l'introduction d'une arme, ou coupe-papier, pour établir la prise de possession" (p. 381). And we recall again the "*Virginité* qui . . . elle-même s'est comme *divisée* en ses fragments de candeur" (p. 387).

11
L'ECCLÉSIASTIQUE

In an early poem, *Renouveau*, Mallarmé experienced "le printemps" as "maladif,"[1] contrasted with "l'hiver, saison de l'art serein." Here, the winter is, rather, a time of "ironie" and "équivoque," and spring is characterized by the opposite: "un naturalisme absolu ou naïf."

To the extent that art is unnatural (even a "serene" art), the latter view seems consistent with the first, but obviously there is something arbitrary about the distinction: one can find wholeness and simple goodness in winter sports, for example. It generally depends on what you do as well as your temper. In the present case, it is gratifying to see Mallarmé writing in a mood which is so universal and normal. He enjoys seeing the priest getting "immediate" pleasure out of rolling on the lawn, "happier than a donkey." All this, of course, refutes the standard views about Mallarmé's abstractness; Sartre nicely answered that those who saw in him only Platonic ideas were "either dupes or knaves."[2] But this is not the place to argue that.

The prose poetry is close in texture to that of Baudelaire in the *Spleen de Paris*, and on the whole unproblematic. At the end, Mallarmé speaks of this "image marquée d'un sceau mystérieux de modernité, à la fois baroque et belle." "Baroque," here, as in the traditional French acceptation, is merely "bizarre", but it is consonant with the important aspect of tension or contrast – even the grotesque – in the historical Baroque as we now understand it.

The "modernité" is typical of Mallarmé's brand of it, rather like Joyce's or Eliot's: he enjoyed the observation of contemporary events *sub specie aeternitatis*, which makes for amusingly jarring syncopations – the priest, with his ancient religious tradition (and, behind that, the "texte inscrit dans sa chair," far more ancient physical and biological laws which determine his impulses) carried on in a contemporary setting, Paris, and specifically the recently set up ("d'hier") Bois de Boulogne.

The ancient–modern tension is pleasantly oxymoronic, "Baroque," in much the same way as Ulysses in twentieth-century Dublin was for Joyce, or the Convent of the Sacred Heart *versus* Sweeney for T. S. Eliot. Mallarmé worked out these sweeping perspectives more thoroughly in his late essays, "Catholicisme" and "De même," as well as the fragments of *Le Livre* and their subsequent fruition in the *Coup de Dés*.

The old–new dialectic is in a polypolar network: head–feet, art–nature, intelligence–simplicity, and so on; that clear web of syntax gives a neat roundedness to the little piece.

L'Ecclésiastique

Les printemps poussent l'organisme à des actes qui, dans une autre saison, lui sont inconnus et maint traité d'histoire naturelle abonde en descriptions de ce phénomène, chez les animaux. Qu'il serait d'un intérêt plus plausible de recueillir certaines des altérations qu'apporte l'instant climatérique dans les allures d'individus faits pour la spiritualité! Mal quitté par l'ironie de l'hiver, j'en retiens, quant à moi, un état équivoque tant que ne s'y substitue pas un naturalisme absolu ou naïf, capable de poursuivre une jouissance dans la différenciation de plusieurs brins d'herbes. Rien dans le cas actuel n'apportant de profit à la foule, j'échappe, pour le méditer, sous quelques ombrages environnant d'hier la ville: or c'est de leur mystère presque banal que j'exhiberai un exemple saisissable et frappant des inspirations printanières.

Vive fut tout à l'heure, dans un endroit peu fréquenté du bois de Boulogne, ma surprise quand, sombre agitation basse, je vis, par les mille interstices d'arbustes bons à ne rien cacher, total et des battements supérieurs de tricorne s'animant jusqu'à des souliers affermis par des boucles en argent, un ecclésiastique, qui à l'écart de témoins, répondait aux sollicitations du gazon. A moi ne plût (et rien de pareil ne sert les desseins providentiels) que, coupable à l'égal d'un faux scandalisé se saisissant d'un caillou du chemin, j'amenasse par mon sourire même d'intelligence, une rougeur sur le visage à deux mains voilé de ce pauvre homme, autre que celle sans doute trouvée dans son solitaire exercice! Le pied vif, il me fallut, pour ne produire par ma présence de distraction, user d'adresse; et fort contre la tentation d'un regard porté en arrière, me figurer en esprit l'apparition quasi diabolique qui continuait à froisser le renouveau de ses côtes, à droite, à gauche et du ventre, en obtenant une chaste frénésie. Tout, se frictionner ou jeter les membres, se rouler, glisser, aboutissait à une satisfaction: et s'arrêter, interdit du chatouillement de quelque haute tige de fleur à de noirs mollets, parmi cette robe spéciale portée avec l'apparence qu'on est pour soi tout même sa femme. Solitude, froid silence épars dans la verdure, perçus par des sens moins subtils qu'inquiets, vous connûtes les claquements furibonds d'une étoffe; comme si la nuit absconse en ses plis en sortait enfin secouée! et les heurts sourds contre la terre du squelette rajeuni; mais l'énergumène n'avait point à vous contempler. Hilare, c'était assez de chercher en soi la cause d'un plaisir ou d'un devoir, qu'expliquait mal un retour, devant une pelouse, aux gambades du séminaire. L'influence du souffle vernal doucement dilatant les immuables textes inscrits en sa chair, lui aussi, enhardi de ce trouble agréable à sa stérile pensée, était venu reconnaître par un contact avec la Nature, immédiat, net, violent, positif, dénué de toute curiosité intellectuelle, le bien-être général; et candidement, loin des obédiences et de la contrainte de son occupation, des canons, des interdits, des censures, il se roulait, dans la béatitude de sa simplicité native, plus heureux qu'un âne. Que le but de sa promenade atteint se soit, droit et d'un jet, relevé non sans secouer les pistils et essuyer les sucs attachés à sa personne, le héros de ma vision, pour rentrer, inaperçu, dans la foule, et les habitudes de son ministère, je ne songe à rien nier; mais j'ai le droit de ne point considérer cela. Ma récompense d'en fixer à jamais comme une rêverie de passant se plut à la compléter, l'image marquée d'un sceau mystérieux de modernité, à la fois baroque et belle?

The Ecclesiatic

The spring seasons impel the organism to acts which, in another season, are unknown to it, and many a treatise of natural history abounds in descriptions of this phenomenon, among animals. Of how much more plausible interest it would be to gather some of the changes which the climateric instant brings about in the demeanor of individuals made for spirituality! The irony of winter hardly having left me, I retain of it, for my own part, an equivocal state as long as it is not replaced by a naïve or absolute naturalism, capable of pursuing enjoyment in the differentiation of several blades of grass. Nothing in the present case bringing profit to the crowd, I escape, in order to meditate on it, beneath some shades surrounding the city as of late: now it is from within their almost banal mystery that I shall exhibit a graspable and striking example of vernal inspirations.

Keen was my surprise as just now, in a seldom-frequented spot of the Bois de Boulogne, when I saw, somber low agitation, through the thousand interstices of bushes good for hiding nothing, entire and exciting himself from the upper palpitations of the tricorn hat down to the shoes fastened by silver buckles, an ecclesiastic who, far from witnesses, was responding to the solicitations of the lawn. Far be it from me (and nothing similar serves the designs of providence) that, guilty as a scandalized hypocrite seizing a pebble from the road, I should bring, by my smile even of understanding, a blush upon this poor man's face covered with both hands, other than that doubtless found in his solitary exercise! Fast of foot, I had to use some skill in order not to produce a distraction by my presence; and steeled against the temptation of a backward glance, imagine in my mind the quasi-diabolical apparition who went on rumpling the vernal renewal, with his sides, on the right, on the left, and with his stomach, while achieving a chaste frenzy. Everything, rubbing himself or throwing his limbs about, rolling, sliding, led to a satisfaction: and stopping, bewildered by some tall flower stem tickling his black calves, amid that special gown worn with the appearance that one is everything for oneself, even one's own wife. Solitude, cold silence scattered in the greenery, perceived by senses less subtle than troubled, you have known a cloth's furious slappings; as if the night hidden in its folds came finally shaken out of it! and the dull thuds against the earth of the rejuvenated skeleton; but the possessed one did not have to contemplate you at all. It was enough to seek in himself mirthfully the cause of a pleasure or a duty, which was hardly explained by a return to the capers of the seminary upon seeing a lawn. The influence of the spring-time breath gently expanding the immutable texts inscribed in his flesh, he too, emboldened by this confusion agreeable to his sterile thought, had come to acknowlege the general well-being by an immediate clear, violent, positive contact with Nature, free of any intellectual curiosity; and candidly, far from the servitudes and constraints of his occupation, from canons, interdicts or censures, he was rolling, in the beatitude of his native simplicity, happier than a donkey. That, the object of his promenade attained, the hero of my vision got up straight at once, not without shaking off the pistils and wiping off the sap clinging to his person, in order to return unnoticed into the crowd and the habits of his ministry, I do not dream of denying it; but I have the right not to take that into

consideration. My discretion with regard to incipiently beheld
frolics does it not receive for its reward to fix thereof forever, as a
passer-by's reverie enjoyed to completing it, the image marked
with a mysterious seal of modernity, at once baroque and
beautiful?   ◄§

As in the case of *Un Spectacle interrompu*, Mallarmé, like Ber-
diayev, plumps for the *truly exceptional* event which somehow
opens up a chink to deep understanding. Springtime pushes
animals – and, by extension, people – to unusual acts, but in
"individuals made for spirituality" this process seems particularly
worth observing.

Mallarmé then makes his (arbitrary) point about winter's irony
and spring's naïve simplicity as we go back to Nature: *Oh rus
quando te.* This *nostos* was the gravamen of the essay "Bucolique":
"La première en date, la nature . . . communiquait à ma jeunesse
une ferveur que je dis passion . . . " (p. 402).

All of our progress loops back that way; like a river seen from a
train:

Toute fuite plus en avant, revient en tant que fleuve   (p. 404)

Rien ne transgresse les figures du val, du pré, de l'arbre   (p. 404)

Mallarmé in this sees Nature as prolonged in the best art, together
contrasted with contemporary herd restlessness and mediocrity.
This theme will be further developed in *La Gloire*: especially in
autumn, with its hints of total Return, a man is humbled into his
proper place in the cosmic scheme. Mallarmé is nothing if not
rooted; "Earthy Mallarmé," the title of my recent essay, acknow-
ledges the importance of this trait. "Bucolique" concludes with this:

Je dis combien, sur les remparts, tonne, peu loin, le canon de l'actualité:
que le bruit puisse cesser à une si faible distance pour qui coupe, en
imagination, un flûte où nouer sa joie selon divers motifs celui, surtout, de
se percevoir, simple, infiniment sur la terre.

In *L'Ecclésiastique*, the return is somewhat milder, though still
"eternal": there is more humor and distancing; the contemporary is
less directly scored, and gently enters into the fun rather like the
"Plumtrees Potted Meat" signs in Joyce.

Since, Mallarmé says at the outset, the "crowd" would not be
interested in his unusual anecdote, he goes to meditate on it alone
under the newly-established foliage partly surrounding the city –

the Bois de Boulogne – and the almost banal mystery in the shadowy leaves of such public trees is the site of his little scene.

A while before, behind the bushes which, scattered, hide nothing, he saw the priest frisking in the grass, shaking from his three-cornered hat down to his buckled shoes.[3] The poet, ever polite, understanding, was very careful not to embarrass him by revealing his presence (even if he smiled sympathetically) and so took off, without looking back. He had to imagine the rest: the continued self-massage all over bringing a "chaste frenzy." These vivacious movements gave the "poor man" satisfaction, and would stop only if some tall flower stem tickled his black-clad calves amidst the robe – that badge of celibacy indicating that in this calling one is beyond sexual differentiation.

The theme of androgeneity associated with the spiritual is widespread in Mallarmé:[4] there is the ambiguous siren figure of the final poet in the *Coup de Dés*, the concept of Ophelia as the "objectified youth" of Hamlet in the essay on him, the self-sufficient complexity of Hérodiade, and so on. He refers, partly jocosely, to his soul as "une si exquise dame anormale" (p. 293).

The solitude and silence witnessed the flappings of the agitated cloth. A remark that this silence was perceived by "senses less subtle than disquieted" means, no doubt, that the priest's encounter with the integrity of Nature was not the awed quiet communion which Romantic and Symbolist poets were apt to portray, and which one might have expected of a man of the cloth, and that is made clear in the phrase "the possessed one did not have to contemplate you at all."

The "night shaken from the folds" is an image which Mallarmé has explored elsewhere,[5] implying a metaphysical entity as deep as Nature: the original darkness of any pit. By extension, it is the metaphysical darkness of original mysteries as expounded by the Church: the folds of cloth are analogous to the folds of sacred text as well as those of the brain. Mallarmé enjoyed this play of ideas between text and its etymological root *texere*, to weave (cloth) in many images, such as "ce pli de sombre dentelle qui retient l'infini, tissé par mille" (p. 1565), referring to writing: *Une dentelle s'abolit*[6] and *Salut* are largely based on these analogies. This is developed in the opening pages of the *Coup de Dés*, in the womb–wave–trough image, which gradually becomes the rhythm of writing, and we recall the *ombre* hidden in the skirts of the mysterious lady in *Le Nénuphar blanc*, a similar source of art.

These profound notions go with the priestly function, of course, in Mallarmé's meditative conception of that role as expressed in "Catholicisme" and "De même." But the priest, we recall, was not looking in the direction of silent natural *shadows* or his kindred robe's *darkness* this free day: only rather, in his pagan sensual self for the "pleasure or the duty" to roll in the grass. Nor was he looking in the direction of his own past youth in the seminary with its probable bouts of horse-play on its lawns. No, it was spring's effect, "dilating the immutable text inscribed in his flesh," which renewed his usual tired official doctrine through a return to "the world as a book," the spontaneous old laws which *ab origine* make us up before any writing, as we follow in the *anciens calculs* of the *Coup de Dés* (page 4). It is the "livre de lui-même" in which Hamlet reads as he walks through the essay on him. But in this instance the emphasis is purely pagan and uncomplicated, having to do with the "general well-being" of all mankind, the salutary effect of letting go. It has been observed on occasion that Nature is not simple, but relative to our frantic manipulations, the complications of struggle against fate; it often seems so as we relax, let go to momentarily easier circumstances amid greenery, water, weather.

Mallarmé goes on to picture his getting up and brushing himself off and returning to his routine existence, but he adds that he need not go into that. His discretion, we were given to feel, in hastening off after a brief glimpse of the intimate scene merits an artist's reward: the loss in ordinary completeness horizontally – the flow of events – is made up for in the *depth* of creative definition which completes the vision on its own terms, and, like Gautier's *buste*, lasts. Mallarmé's parting "à jamais" is no doubt somewhat ironic and "bombastic" – inflated on purpose – given the modesty of the enterprise.

But the game was worth the candle: the style, the composition, are notably tight and apposite. Like the crowd in *La Déclaration foraine*, we do not leave this little *skéné*[7] feeling cheated.

12

LA GLOIRE

Mallarmé's biggest creative problem was like that of the inventor of the combustion engine: how to tame his explosive genius, how to convert its monstrously swelling "mushroom cloud" into the rhythmic put-puts of craft. Original nature had similar problems, one guesses, converting the Big Bang into articulate evolution.[1]

Prose (*pour des Esseintes*) tells of a major youthful phase of the *agon*, and Mallarmé's smiling *anima* side which saved him for on-going life. "Patience," the key word of the poem, succeeded in getting the genie back into the bottle. The repeated *trop* of that decisive poem – a main step leading to the *Grand Œuvre* – along with the same usage in the *Correspondance* of the early crucial period and the "trop . . . en opposition au ciel" – Promethean hubris – of the *Coup de Dés* is sufficient commentary.[2]

Patience means not only painstaking gradualism in work habits but a whole set of attitudes moving one (pivoting) toward the tempered, horizontal, metonymic and gently flowing feminine aspect of existence. Modesty, learning to laugh at one's pretences, heeding the wisely admonitory and consoling feminine smile, getting involved in other people or things, a general "living it down," were all part of that desperately necessary inner stance, as we perceive from those stormy, exalted adolescent letters.

Poem after poem: *Le Pitre châtié*, *Victorieusement fui*, *Quelconque une solitude*, *Quelle soie*, the essay "Bucolique," and, importantly for us now, *La Gloire*, celebrate victories in this lifelong survival process; survival of the person and of the works as humanly possible expressions. Often in these poems, as in *Prose* (*pour des Esseintes*) Mallarmé turns spontaneously to the feminine – patience is signally woman's – as the key and way of on-going life. So does the later Goethe; his *Ewig-Weibliche* was essentially this river of "concatenation" (*The Elective Affinities*).

In *La Gloire*, the pivoting is away from the usual temptation and sin of vain-glory toward a revelling in "mere" existence and humanity as a creature among creatures, privileged to be "simple, infiniment sur la terre" ("Bucolique," p. 405).

The fact that he revels *alone* is a reminder of man's incorrigible ironies. One may think of the majestic trees he reviews gratefully in his familiar *forêt de Fontainebleau* as his fellow-creatures, standing perhaps for other individual glories among his forbears, helping him find a "modest" place among others, rather in the spirit of Dante saying "they made me one of them." That too is ambiguous, incorrigibly complex as reality is. Even the Trinity was a sort of elite club, according to Northrop Frye. Wordsworth's *Prelude* ends on just this proud–modest note. So there is a specialness in this commonness with quasi-divine tall beings, and in turning his back – as Wordsworth did – on the hustling city of men he has left behind at the Gare Saint-Lazare, and this makes for a special exultation. After all, it is only *ordinary* glory[3] he rejects, "la gloriole"; in this he is one with all true artists. So in the end we have a very problematic modesty. Those powerful needs which soon seem like all-too-human ploys work only for a while, and Mallarmé knew it, as did the creator of *Notes from Underground*. Old reversibilities are at work down there. The "gloire du long désir"[4] will eventually out, and fittingly does so in this last prose poem of the original collection. *Conflit*, which was added later, easily prolongs this mood of cosmic reconciliation.

We come into this world "trailing clouds of glory" (Wordsworth, *Ode on the Intimations of Immortality*), and Mallarmé often thought of exiting the same way, definitely not with a whimper but a passionate bang, Edenic in revelation and beauty. So he conceived the "moment de foudre" of his Saint Jean. And so in a way would his own life end as he exploded into a vision – "Ne trouvez-vous pas que c'est un acte de démence?" – of an ambitious masterpiece represented at least partially by the *Coup de Dés*.

Gide commented[5] that only the very greatest artists end this way: Beethoven with his late quartets, Joyce with his *Finnegans Wake*. And we might add Goethe, Yeats, Eliot . . .

We have only a foretaste of that outcome in this quietly glowing little piece, which is discreet, humorous, very human and patient. But for those of us who know what the outcome would be, it is movingly suggestive.

❧ La Gloire

La Gloire! je ne la sus qu'hier, irréfragable, et rien ne m'intéressera d'appelé par quelqu'un ainsi.

Cent affiches s'assimilant l'or incompris des jours, trahison de la lettre, ont fui, comme à tous confins de la ville, mes yeux au ras de l'horizon par un départ sur le rail traînés avant de se recueillir dans l'abstruse fierté que donne une approche de forêt en son temps d'apothéose.

Si discord parmi l'exaltation de l'heure, un cri faussa ce nom connu pour déployer la continuité de cimes tard évanouies, Fontainebleau que je pensai, la glace du compartiment violentée, du poing aussi étreindre à la gorge l'interrupteur: Tais-toi! Ne divulgue pas du fait d'un aboi indifférent l'ombre ici insinuée dans mon esprit, aux portières de wagons battant sous un vent inspiré et égalitaire, les touristes omniprésents vomis. Une quiétude menteuse de riches bois suspend alentour quelque extraordinaire état d'illusion, que me réponds-tu? qu'ils ont, ces voyageurs, pour ta gare aujourd'hui quitté la capitale, bon employé vociférateur par devoir et dont je n'attends, loin d'accaparer une ivresse à tous départie par les libéralités conjointes de la nature et de l'Etat, rien qu'un silence prolongé le temps de m'isoler de la délégation urbaine vers l'extatique torpeur de ces feuillages là-bas trop immobilisés pour qu'une crise ne les éparpille bientôt dans l'air; voici, sans attenter à ton intégrité, tiens, une monnaie.

Un uniforme inattentif m'invitant vers quelque barrière, je remets sans dire mot, au lieu du suborneur métal, mon billet.

Obéi pourtant, oui, à ne voir que l'asphalte s'étaler net de pas, car je ne peux encore imaginer qu'en ce pompeux octobre exceptionnel du million d'existences étageant leur vacuité en tant qu'une monotonie énorme de capitale dont va s'effacer ici la hantise avec le coup de sifflet sous la brume, aucun furtivement évadé que moi n'ait senti qu'il est, cet an, d'amers et lumineux sanglots, mainte indécise flottaison d'idée désertant les hasards comme des branches, tel frisson et ce qui fait penser à un automne sous les cieux.

Personne et, les bras de doute envolés comme qui porte aussi un lot d'une splendeur secrète, trop inappréciable trophée pour paraître! mais sans du coup m'élancer dans cette diurne veillée d'immortels troncs au déversement sur un d'orgueils surhumains (or ne faut-il pas qu'on en constate l'authenticité?) ni passer le seuil où des torches consument, dans une haute garde, tous rêves antérieurs à leur éclat répercutant en pourpre dans la nue l'universel sacre de l'intrus royal qui n'aura eu qu'à venir: j'attendis, pour l'être, que lent et repris du mouvement ordinaire, se réduisît à ses proportions d'une chimère puérile emportant du monde quelque part, le train qui m'avait là déposé seul. 　　　　　　　　　　　　　　　　　　◅

Glory

Glory! I did not know it until yesterday, irrefragable, and nothing thus called by anyone will interest me.

A hundred signs assimilating the days' misunderstood gold, betrayal of letters, have fled, as at all the confines of the city, my eyes drawn to the level of the horizon by a departure on the rails before communing with the abstruse pride which the approach of a forest gives in its time of apotheosis.

So in discord amidst the hour's exaltation, a cry falsified this name known to unfold the continuity of late vanished tree tops, Fontainebleau, that I thought, the glass of the compartment having been outraged with my fist, also of seizing therewith the interruptor by the throat: Be quiet! Do not divulge by means of an indifferent barking the shadow here insinuated in my mind, to the carriage doors banging under an inspired and egalitarian wind, the omnipresent tourists being spewed out. A deceptive calm of rich woods suspends roundabout some extraordinary state of illusion, what do you answer me? that they, these travelers, have left the capital for your station today, good employee vociferating out of duty, and of whom I expect, far from hoarding an intoxication dispensed to all by the joint liberalities of nature and the State, nothing but a silence prolonged for the time it takes to isolate myself from the urban delegation toward the ecstatic torpor of those leaves yonder, too still but that a crisis will not soon disperse them in the air; see, without making an attempt upon your integrity, take it, a coin.

An inattentive uniform inviting me to some barrier, I hand over, without saying a word, instead of the bribing metal, my ticket.

Obeyed however, yes, in seeing only the asphalt spread out clear of footsteps, for I cannot yet imagine that in this pompous exceptional October, of the million existences stacking up their vacuity as an enormous monotony of the capital, whose obsession is going to become obliterated here with the blast of the whistle in the mist, no one but I stealthily escaped should have felt that there are, this year, bitter and luminous sobs, many a doubtful floating of ideas deserting chance like branches, a certain shiver and which makes one think of an autumn beneath the skies.

No one, doubt's arms flown away as one who also carries a portion of secret splendor, too inappreciable a trophy to appear! but without dashing at once into this diurnal vigil of immortal tree trunks to the pouring out upon one of superhuman prides (for must one not ascertain its authenticity?) nor passing the threshold where torches consume, in a high guard, all dreams anterior to their éclat, reverberating in purple in the clouds the universal consecration of the royal intruder who will only have had to come: I waited, in order to be such a one, that the train, slowly and taken up by its ordinary motion, should be reduced to its proportions of a childish fancy carrying people somewhere, having deposited me there alone.

The piece opens like the *Coup de Dés*, with a dazzling, original sunburst.[6] "La Gloire" is fully Edenic in that sense, initial and final, "Gloire du long désir," and hence a beacon image, miraculously granted in privileged moments such as he has just had that can light us along our Adamic way toward the promise of wholeness.

At the outset, the opposition between a recently discovered true glory and the usual kind is stated peremptorily, and this is continued in the rejection of the city being left behind, with its philistine modern incomprehension symbolized by the "betrayal of the letter" on ugly signboards and posters littering (as they still do) the approaches to Paris. Mallarmé's sense of the sacredness of the alphabet – a "spiritual zodiac" (*Notes*, p. 850) – expressed as early as "L'Art pour tous," is legendary. Betrayal of the letter is indistinguishable, in his organic and anti-dualistic visionary thought, from betrayal of the spirit, suggested here in "the misunderstood gold of days," the sun–source. That forgotten pure origin is a familiar image too, worked into essays like "Or" and poems like *Hommage à Richard Wagner* or the *Ouverture ancienne d'Hérodiade*. James Lawler, in his fine commentary on the piece,[7] suggests that the dark letters absorb, as dark colors do, the misunderstood gold. And he rightly admires the phonostylistics and other effects which convey the initial monotony of the habitual commuting journey, the rising expectation of aesthetic excitement.

But Mallarmé, like Heidegger later, was notoriously loyal to that Source and communed with it elegiacally particularly at sundown and in autumn, in those analogous phases of the parallel tetrapolar cycles of day and year, moments and scenes of the "tragedy of nature" (*Les Dieux antiques*, p. 1169).[8]

The "apotheosis" of the forest of Fontainebleau is double in this sense. The forest with its "abstruse pride" – its nobly, tragically cosmic mood – will concentrate his feelings in that regard. But on the way along the rails his eyes were drawn to the westering sun on the horizon, as a prologue of the drama.

So great was the discord (in this meditation) brought about by the train conductor's bawling out the word "Fontainebleau" that Mallarmé thought of strangling him, with his "fist," after first using it to break through the glass of the compartment door in exasperation. The man seemed to be deliberately trying to provoke that disaster, almost like a "barker."

The "shadow"[9] released or divulgated – paralleled by the opening compartment doors all along the train – from his mind by that bark is partly the suspicion that hordes of tourists will be spewed out on that beauty which he wants to enjoy alone. The "vent inspiré et égalitaire" is the impulse arising in those many random others, the tourists, to see that same beauty.

Whereas an intimate drama lies latent for his deep appreciation in the "quiétude menteuse," the *Götterdämmerung* of a forest about to expire in October – illustrating the poetic illusion, or lie, of all, that Shakespearean "Rien qui est la vérité"[10] – what does he, the conductor, let out with his voice? The banal fact that those tourists have come to this sacred place.

Mallarmé, with his usual decency, does not really want to monopolize it. He was willing to share the "drunkenness" of that beauty which was made available jointly by nature and the State (which kept up the forest preserve). All he expected from the conductor was a silence that would allow him to move off, away from the others, with his mood intact. He thinks of bribing him to shut up. But, realizing that the fellow is just doing his duty – "uniforme inattentif" brings out that impersonality – he instead just gives up his ticket at the gate, as usual.

But he is obeyed anyway, so it seems, upon his seeing only the asphalt stretch out before him, empty of steps (other than his own): i.e. devoid of tourists. He must be succored by some force, for otherwise he cannot imagine how he is the only one to flee the vacuous capital – whose lingering presence is in the train about to depart, with a whistle blast under the mist – in favor of the bitter "shiver" of beauty and the creative stirring of early (dubious, tentative still) imaginative ideas surging from chaos in the contemplative mind, analogous to leaves detaching themselves from the branches in this ambivalently, poetically, vibrantly alive "floating" and "shivering" season. The orphic mutation of nature into art – music in "Bucolique" or various passages on Wagner, or his verbal music as here – demands a love–death union of forest and poet, soon to be consummated.[11]

Tel frisson, which he thought would prompt others to the pilgrimage, is the summing up of the premonition of the drama; it is the same as "whatever makes one think of an autumn under the skies," the alluring promise of the woods in that season and the expansive feelings that it naturally echoes.

"No one"[12] has joined him on the siding; the "arms of doubt" have fled, figurative arms carrying away a certain amount of secret splendor which will never appear in the minds of the imagined others, or, ambiguously, in his own, for it is too petty, this fleeting triumph over others, to be decently retained in his memory.

But he does not immediately dash into the forest, where he anticipates the pouring forth over one, himself – in a sort of anointment or blessing – of those "superhuman prides" of tall trees, making him "one of them" in the Dantean image. In the parenthesis he hesitates, testing the forest against ordinary reality, in a sort of pinching of the self, which recalls the faun's.[13]

There the trees consume in the love–death drama of existential nature all the dreams in the lively but impermanent (hence "float-ing," illusory) leaves which summer brought to a head. This sacrificial moment is pagan–holy, royal as the purple in the declin-ing autumn skies. And by extension the solitary poet and intruder is consecrated, anointed, in his own royalty. All he had to do in *this* kingdom is come.

This rumination was a foretaste. For the full savoring he waited till that last vestige of banality, the train, departed, till it became in its diminishing-with-distance proportions the childish illusion – as opposed to this mature artistic vision which rejected the life–lie, accepted *Sein zum Tode* – of self-importance and bad faith symbo-lized by that modern Ship of Fools, carrying off unwitting folks and leaving him gloriously alone. The whole shape of his life, his vocation, is suggested.

I used the term "pagan–holy" as expressed in Wagner's "sacre",[14] "mon sacre",[15] and the like. Mallarmé's faith, like Camus', is an elusive one, closer to Debussy or Stravinsky (*Sacre du printemps*) than to César Franck. But even the "pantheism" one could naturally invoke needs questioning, because there remains a problem of personal *versus* objective, which is never fully resolved for deeply questioning minds like his.

13
CONFLIT

The title refers to a class struggle of sorts but even more to the contradictory sentiments it sets up in Mallarmé. Their dramatic interplay is structured through a network of interlocking tensions and ambiguities that burgeon out and flower in some of his most masterly prose as well as poetry:

> Cet unanime blanc conflit
> D'une guirlande avec la même
> Enfui contre la vitre blême
> Flotte plus qu'il n'ensevelit   (*Une dentelle s'abolit*)

The location is once again, as in the preceding piece, Valvins and mainly at a window, as often in these – and other – prose poems. Mallarmé has returned to his villa in spring and, pushing back a shutter, discovers his refuge has been invaded by railway workers. He resents the noise and the whole idea of hustling civilization's intrusion into this place of solitude and serenity (in *La Gloire*, the problem was with tourists who were more numerous but less closely invasive).

Mallarmé occupied only a part of the villa, the top floor, and the ground floor had been rented out as a canteen for the workers; the cellar was occupied by their tools. He thinks of at least closing off his little garden. There is a moment of hostile confrontation.[1] But after a while he makes his inner peace with those humble others, seeing them as brother Adams, co-workers on this earth. Contemplating them sprawled in drunken stupor on their Magna Mater, the ground of us all, on their Sunday rest day, he feels they share a common destiny with the poet *sub specie aeternitatis*.

Mallarmé was about as different from these itinerant laborers as two types of humans can be. But he was imaginative generosity itself. He wanted to create a myth for mankind, and in his fragments of *Le Livre* he dreamed of all sorts of ways of overcoming his difference with others, seeking to get beyond his own ego to this transcendent end, perhaps by becoming anonymous.

Paul Bénichou in his "Mallarmé et le public"[2] studies this aspect of the seemingly aloof master symbolist; Jean-Pierre Richard offers a similar perspective in the final pages of *L'Univers imaginaire de Mallarmé*.[3] In my *L'Œuvre de Mallarmé: Un Coup de Dés*, I had offered my own views (particularly in the Conclusion) on this heart-warming side of Mallarmé's genius.

One can observe its roots in the earliest poems, such as *Aumône* where he displays his sympathy for a tramp, a brother outsider. The prose poems have provided us with many examples: the little orphan child of the streets, the juvenile circus performers, and the bear of *Un Spectacle interrompu*, a sort of poor cousin of man who tries to lift himself to understanding and dignity and attracts Mallarmé's compassion, as animals often do for humans generally.

Mid-way in the text, he reflects that he could have bought the place and avoided the problem, but did not do so out of his desire to remain propertyless, free and open to experience, like his disciple Gide (who had less success). In his correspondence with Simone de Beauvoir,[4] Sartre exclaims with enthusiasm about Mallarmé's being so existential – the theme of his later long essay "L'Engagement de Mallarmé" – referring especially to this experiential availability, which he, Sartre, would strive to maintain in his turn.

❧ Conflit

Longtemps, voici du temps – je croyais – que s'exempta mon idée d'aucun accident même vrai; préférant aux hasards, puiser, dans son principe, jaillissement.

Un goût pour une maison abandonnée, lequel paraîtrait favorable à cette disposition, amène à dédire: tant le contentement pareil, chaque année verdissant l'escalier de pierres extérieur, sauf celle-ci, à pousser contre les murailles un volet hivernal puis raccorder comme si pas d'interruption, l'œillade d'à présent au spectacle immobilisé autrefois. Gage de retours fidèles, mais voilà que ce battement vermoulu, scande un vacarme, refrains, altercations, en dessous; je me rappelle comment la légende de la malheureuse demeure dont je hante le coin intact, envahie par une bande de travailleurs en train d'offenser le pays parce que tout de solitude, avec une voie ferrée, survint, m'angoissa au départ, irais-je ou pas, me fit presque hésiter – à revoir, tant pis! ce sera à

défendre, comme mien, arbitrairement s'il faut, le local et j'y suis.
Une tendresse, exclusive dorénavant, que c'ait été lui qui, dans la
suppression concernant des sites précieux, reçût la pire injure;
hôte, je le deviens, de sa déchéance: invraisemblablement, le
séjour chéri pour la désuétude et de l'exception, tourné par les
progrès en cantine d'ouvriers de chemin de fer.

Terrassiers, puisatiers, par qui un velours hâve aux jambes,
semble que le remblai bouge, ils dressent, au repos, dans une
tranchée, la rayure bleu et blanc transversale des maillots comme la
nappe d'eau peu à peu (vêtement oh! que l'homme est la source
qu'il cherche): ce les sont, mes co-locataires jadis ceux, en esprit,
quand je les rencontrai sur les routes, choyés comme les ouvriers
quelconques par excellence: la rumeur les dit chemineaux. Las et
forts, grouillement partout où la terre a souci d'être modifiée, eux
trouvent, en l'absence d'usine, sous les intempéries, indépendance.

Les maîtres si quelque part, dénués de gêne, verbe haut. – Je suis
le malade des bruits et m'étonne que presque tout le monde
répugne aux odeurs mauvaises, moins au cri. Cette cohue entre,
part, avec le manche, à l'épaule, de la pioche et de la pelle: or, elle
invite, en sa faveur, les émotions de derrière la tête et force à
procéder, directement, d'idées dont on se dit *c'est de la littérature!*
Tout à l'heure, dévot ennemi, pénétrant dans une crypte ou cellier
en commun, devant la rangée de l'outil double, cette pelle et cette
pioche, sexuels – dont le métal, résumant la force pure du travail-
leur, féconde les terrains sans culture, je fus pris de religion, outre
que de mécontentement, émue à m'agenouiller. Aucun homme de
loi ne se targue de déloger l'intrus – baux tacites, usages locaux –
établi par surprise et ayant même payé aux propriétaires: je dois
jouer le rôle ou restreindre, à mes droits, l'empiètement. Quelque
langage, la chance que je le tienne, comporte du dédain, bien sûr,
puisque la promiscuité, couramment, me déplaît: ou, serai-je d'une
note juste, conduit à discourir ainsi? – Camarades – par exemple –
vous ne supposez pas l'état de quelqu'un épars dans un paysage
celui-ci, où toute foule s'arrête, en tant qu'épaisseur de forêt à
l'isolement que j'ai voulu tutélaire de l'eau; or mon cas, tel et,
quand on jure, hoquète, se bat et s'estropie, la discordance
produit, comme dans ce suspens lumineux de l'air, la plus intolé-
rable si sachez, invisible des déchirures. – Pas que je redoute
l'inanité, quant à des simples, de cet aveu, qui les frapperait,
sûrement, plus qu'autres au monde et ne commanderait le même
rire immédiat qu'à onze messieurs, pour voisins: avec le sens,
pochards, du merveilleux et, soumis à une rude corvée, de délica-

tesses quelque part supérieures, peut-être ne verraient-ils, dans mon douloureux privilège, aucune démarcation strictement sociale pour leur causer ombrage, mais personnelle – s'observeraient-ils un temps, bref, l'habitude plausiblement reprend le dessus; à moins qu'un ne répondit, tout de suite, avec égalité. – Nous, le travail cessé pour un peu, éprouvons le besoin de se confondre, entre soi: qui a hurlé, moi, lui? son coup de voix m'a grandi, et tiré de la fatigue, aussi est-ce, déjà, boire, gratuitement, d'entendre crier un autre. – Leur chœur, incohérent, est en effet nécessaire. Comme vite je me relâche de ma défense, avec la même sensibilité qui l'aiguisa; et j'introduis, par la main, l'assaillant. Ah! à l'exprès et propre usage du rêveur se clôture, au noir d'arbres, en spacieux retirement, la Propriété, comme veut le vulgaire: il faut que je l'aie manquée, avec obstination, durant mes jours – omettant le moyen d'acquisition – pour satisfaire quelque singulier instinct de ne rien posséder et de seulement passer, au risque d'une résidence comme maintenant ouverte à l'aventure qui n'est pas, tout à fait, le hasard, puisqu'il me rapproche, selon que je me fis, de prolétaires.

Alternatives, je prévois la saison, de sympathie et de malaise . . .

– Ou souhaiterais, pour couper court, qu'un me cherchât querelle: en attendant et seule stratégie, s'agit de clore un jardinet, sablé, fleuri par mon art, en terrasse sur l'onde, la pièce d'habitation à la campagne . . . Qu'étranger ne passe le seuil, comme vers un cabaret, les travailleurs iront à leur chantier par un chemin loué et fauché dans les moissons.

"Fumier!" accompagné de pieds dans la grille, se profère violemment: je comprends qui l'aménité nomme, eh! bien même d'un soûlaud, grand gars le visage aux barreaux, elle me vexe malgré moi; est-ce caste, du tout, je ne mesure, individu à individu, de différence, en ce moment, et ne parviens à ne pas considérer le forcené, titubant et vociférant, comme un homme ou à nier le ressentiment à son endroit. Très raide, il me scrute avec animosité. Impossible de l'annuler, mentalement: de parfaire l'œuvre de la boisson, le coucher, d'avance, en la poussière et qu'il ne soit pas ce colosse tout à coup grossier et méchant. Sans que je cède même par un pugilat qui illustrerait, sur le gazon, la lutte des classes, à ses nouvelles provocations débordantes. Le mal qui le ruine, l'ivrognerie, y pourvoira, à ma place, au point que le sachant, je souffre de mon mutisme, gardé indifférent, qui me fait complice.

Un énervement d'états contradictoires, oiseux, faussés et la contagion jusqu'à moi, par du trouble, de quelque imbécile ébriété.

Même le calme, obligatoire dans une région d'échos, comme on y trempe, je l'ai, particulièrement les soirs de dimanche, jusqu'au silence. Appréhension quant à cette heure, qui prend la transparence de la journée, avant les ombres puis l'écoule lucide vers quelque profondeur. J'aime assister, en paix, à la crise et qu'elle se réclame de quelqu'un. Les compagnons apprécient l'instant, à leur façon, se concertent entre souper et coucher, sur les salaires ou interminablement disputent, en le décor vautrés. M'abstraire ni quitter, exclus, la fenêtre, regard, moi là, de l'ancienne bâtisse sur l'endroit qu'elle sait; pour faire au groupe des avances, sans effet. Toujours le cas: pas lieu de se trouver ensemble; un contact peut, je le crains, n'intervenir entre des hommes. – "Je dis" une voix "que nous trimons, chacun ici, au profit d'autres." – "Mieux," interrompais-je bas, "vous le faites, afin qu'on vous paie et d'être légalement, quant à vous seuls." – "Oui, les bourgeois," j'entends, peu concerné, "veulent un chemin de fer". – "Pas moi, du moins" pour sourire "je ne vous ai pas appelés dans cette contrée de luxe et sonore, bouleversée autant que je suit gêné." Ce colloque, fréquent, en muettes restrictions de mon côté, manque, par enchantement; quelle pierrerie, le ciel fluide! Toutes les bouches ordinaires tues au ras du sol comme y dégorgeant leur vanité de parole. J'allais conclure: "Peut-être, moi aussi, je travaille . . ." – A quoi? n'eût objecté aucun, admettant, à cause de compatables, l'occupation transférée des bras à la tête. A quoi – tait, dans la conscience seule, un écho – du moins, qui puisse servir, parmi l'échange général. Tristesse que ma production reste, à ceux-ci, par essence, comme les nuages au crépuscule ou des étoiles, vaine.

Véritablement, aujourd'hui, qu'y a-t-il?

L'escouade du labeur git au rendez-vous mais vaincue. Ils ont trouvé, l'un après l'autre qui la forment, ici affalée en l'herbe, l'élan à peine, chancelant tous comme sous un projectile, d'arriver et tomber à cet étroit champ de bataille: quel sommeil de corps contre la motte sourde.

Ainsi vais-je librement admirer et songer.

Non, ma vue ne peut, de l'ouverture où je m'accoude, s'échapper dans la direction de l'horizon, sans que quelque chose de moi n'enjambe, indûment, avec manque d'égard et de convenance à mon tour, cette jonchée d'un fléau; dont, en ma qualité, je dois comprendre le mystère et juger le devoir: car, contrairement à la majorité et beaucoup de plus fortunés, le pain ne lui a pas suffi – ils ont peiné une partie notable de la semaine, pour l'obtenir d'abord; et, maintenant, la voici, demain, ils ne savent pas, rampent par le vague et piochent sant mouvement – qui fait en son sort, un trou égal à celui creusé, jusqu'ici, tous les jours, dans la réalité des terrains (fondation, certes, de temple). Ils réservent, honorablement, sans témoigner de ce que c'est ni que s'éclaire cette fête, la part du sacré dans l'existence, par un arrêt, l'attente et le momentané suicide. La connaissance qui resplendirait – d'un orgueil inclus à l'ouvrage journalier, résister, simplement et se montrer debout – alentour magnifiée par une colonnade de futaie; quelque instinct la chercha dans un nombre considérable, pour les déjeter ainsi, de petits verres et ils en sont, avec l'absolu d'un accomplissement rituel, moins officiants que victimes, à figurer, au soir, l'hébétement de tâches si l'observance relève de la fatalité plus que d'un vouloir.

Les constellations s'initient à briller: comme je voudrais que parmi l'obscurité qui court sur l'aveugle troupeau, aussi des points de clarté, telle pensée tout à l'heure, se fixassent, malgré ces yeux scellés ne les distinguant pas – pour le fait, pour l'exactitude, pour qu'il soit dit. Je penserai, donc, uniquement, à eux, les importuns, qui me ferment, par leur abandon, le lointain vespéral; plus que, naguères, par leur tumulte. Ces artisans de tâches élémentaires, il m'est loisible, les veillant, à côté d'un fleuve limpide continu, d'y regarder le peuple – une intelligence robuste de la condition humaine leur courbe l'échine journellement pour tirer, sans l'intermédiaire du blé, le miracle de vie qui assure la présence: d'autres ont fait les défrichements passés et des aqueducs ou livreront un terre-plein à telle machine, les mêmes, Louis-Pierre, Martin, Poitou et le Normand, quand ils ne dorment pas, ainsi s'évoquent-ils selon les mères ou la province; mais plutôt des naissances sombrèrent en l'anonymat et l'immense sommeil l'ouïe à la génératrice, les prostrant, cette fois, subit un accablement et un élargissement de tous les siècles et, autant cela possible – réduite aux proportions sociales, d'éternité.

Conflict

For a long time, its been a time now – I believed – that my thought abstained from any accident even a true one; preferring over chance to plumb, in its principle, for a fountainhead.

A predilection for an abandoned house, which would seem to favor this state of mind, leads me to retract myself: so much is the contentment the same, except this go-around, as each year turns the outside stone stairs green, at pushing wintry shutters back against the walls, then linking as though there had been no interruption, today's glance with the scene formerly immobilized. This is the reward for faithful returns; but now the banging of the worm-eaten shutters scans a racket, refrains and altercations from below; I remember now how the legend of the unfortunate abode, of which I frequent the intact corner, having been invaded by a band of workers engaged in offending the country, because it was till now totally secluded, with a railway, arrived and distressed me at my departure, would I go or not, made me almost hesitate. To see it again, so much the worse! the place will have to be defended as mine, arbitrarily if necessary, and here I am. A tenderness, henceforth exclusive, that it was it which, in the suppression involving handsome places, suffered the greatest insult; I become the host of its decline: unbelievably, the abode cherished for its disuse and exceptionality has been turned by progress into a canteen for railway workers.

Diggers, well-sinkers, through whom, with the corduroy on their legs worn out, the embankment must be going ahead; they line up, at rest in a trench, the blue and white transverse stripes of their jerseys gradually forming like the sheet of water (clothing oh! indicating that man is the source which he is seeking): it is they, my co-tenants formerly those, in my mind, when I encountered them on the roads, coddled like random working men par excellence: reportedly they are itinerant workers. Weary and strong, a swarming mass everywhere where the earth is changed, they find in the absence of a factory, weather's inclemency, their independence.

The masters, if they are around somewhere, free of constraint, are loud of speech. – I am the invalid of noise and am astonished that almost everyone is repelled by bad odors and less so by shouting. This mob enters and leaves with the handles of the picks and shovels on their shoulders: now it invites in its favor emotions in the back of one's mind and forces one to proceed, directly, from ideas of which one says to oneself *that is literature*! Just now, making my way, as a devout enemy, into a crypt or common storage room, before the row of the double tool, this sexual shovel and pick – whose metal, summing up the pure strength of the worker, fecundates the uncultivated soil, I was seized by religion, besides discontent, moved to the point of kneeling down. No man of law prides himself on ousting the intruder – silent leases, local customs – established by surprise and having even paid the owners: I must play the role or restrict, to my rights, the trespass. No matter what language, assuming I were to speak, would sound disdainful, of course, since promiscuousness, now general, displeases me: or will

I be led to speechifying, in the right tone, thus? "comrades" for example, "you cannot imagine the condition of someone dispersed in a landscape such as this, where no crowds penetrate, because of the forest's density, to the isolation which I intended to be the water's guardian; now my position is such, and when there is swearing, hiccuping, fighting and mangling one another, the dissonance produces, as in this luminous uncertainty of the air, the most intolerable, know this, and invisible of tearings." Not that I fear the futility, as regards these unsophisticated people, of this avowal, which would strike them, surely, more than it would others in the world and would not command the same immediate laughter that it would of eleven gentlemen, for neighbors: drunkards, they have a sense for the marvelous and, subject to arduous drudgery, for in some way superior difficulties; and they would in my sorrowful privilege perhaps not see any strictly social demarcation at which to take offense, but a personal one – should they be circumspect for a while, shortly, habit plausibly gets the upper hand again; unless one of them answered, at once, on equal terms. "We feel, when work has stopped for a short time, the need to intermingle with each other: who yelled, me, he? his shout has magnified me, and drawn me out of my weariness; also, it is already like drinking for nothing to hear another shouting." Their incoherent chorus is, as a matter of fact, necessary. And I relax my defense as quickly, with the same sensitiveness which had sharpened it; and I introduce the besieger with my own hand. Ah! for the express and proper use of the dreamer lies enclosed, in the trees' shades, in spacious retirement, the Property, as the vulgar would have it: it must be that I let that chance go by, with obstinacy, in my time – not to mention the means of acquisition – in order to satisfy some peculiar instinct not to possess anything and to merely pass, at the risk of a residence like this one now open to adventure, which is not altogether chance, since it draws me near, according to my development, to proletarians.

Alternatives, I foresee the season of sympathy and uneasiness . . .

– Or would I wish, in order to put an end to this, that someone tried to pick a quarrel: while undecided and as only strategy, it is a question of closing a small garden, graveled, and adorned with flowers by my art, an embanked garden above the water, the country living room . . . May no stranger pass its threshold, as to a tavern, the workers shall go to their workyard by a rented road, mowed in the fields.

"Dungheap," someone shouts violently, accompanied by kicking against the iron gate: I understand who the compliment is aimed at, well, even from a drunkard, a tall fellow with his face against the fence railing, it annoys me despite myself; is it class-consciousness? not at all; I do not, at this moment, individual against individual, measure any difference and do not succeed in not considering the staggering and yelling madman as a man, nor do I succeed in denying my resentment toward him. Very stiff, he scrutinizes me with animosity. Impossible to cancel him, mentally: to finish off the work of drink, to bring him down, first, into the dust, that he might not be this sudden coarse and malevolent giant. I do not even yield to his new provocations which are brimming over, by a fistfight which would illustrate the class struggle on the lawn. The evil which is his ruin, drunkenness, will take care of that for me, to the point that, knowing it, I suffer from my mutism, having remained indifferent, which makes me an accomplice.

An indolent nervous irritation, due to conflicting states of mind, and the contagion, through which the confusion, of some imbecile intoxication, have even gotten to me.

But tranquillity also, which is obligatory in a region of echoes, as one steeps in it, I have it, particularly on Sunday evenings, to the point of silence. I have an apprehension with respect to this hour, which takes on the day's transparency, before the coming of darkness, then disperses it lucidly into some depth. I love to be present, peacefully, at the crisis, that it call someone to witness. The fellows appreciate the moment in their own way and discuss peacefully salaries between supper and bedtime, or dispute interminably, sprawled in the scenery. I do not remove myself, nor leave, though an excluded one, the window of the ancient house which looks out on a familiar place, in order to make advances to the group, without effect. Always this is the case: there is no way of coming together; I fear that it is possible for a contact not to take place among men. "I say," says a voice, "that we are drudging all of us here, for the benefit of others." "What's more," I interrupt under my breath, "you do it in order to be paid and to exist, as far as you are concerned, legally." "Yes, the bourgeois," I hear, not much concerned, "want a railroad." "Not me, at least," having to smile, "I did not call you into this sonorous and luxurious region, which is now thrown into as much of a confusion as I myself am inconvenienced." This frequent colloquy, consisting of silent reservations on my part, is silenced, by magic: what a jewelry, this fluid sky! All common mouths silenced now are flush with the earth, as

120

though they were disgorging their proud oratory there. I was going to conclude: "Perhaps I, too, work ..." No one would have objected "At what?", admitting, on account of pay-masters, the work transferred from the arms to the head. "At what?", an echo, in the consciousness only, falls silent – that might be useful, at least, in the general exchange. I feel a sadness that my production should remain, for these men, in essence, vain like the clouds at twilight or stars.

In truth, what is the matter today?

The work gang lies at the meeting place, but vanquished. They who make it up have found, one after another, here fallen in the grass, hardly the strength, all of them staggering as if shot, to arrive and fall down on this narrow battlefield: what a heavy sleep of bodies on the dull sod.

So I am going to contemplate and muse freely.

No, my view cannot, from the window where I am leaning my elbows, escape in the horizon's direction, without some part of me unduly stepping over these strewn remains of a plague, lacking respect and manners in my turn; I must, in my capacity, understand its mystery and judge its task; for, contrary to the majority and more fortunate of men, bread alone was not enough for them – they have toiled a considerable part of the week, in order to obtain it, first; and now, here they are, they don't know tomorrow and crawl through dimness, digging without movement – which in their destiny makes a hole equal to the one dug, up to now, every day, in the reality of plots of ground (a foundation, most certainly, of a temple). They reserve, honorably, without bearing witness to what it is or without this feast's lightning, the sacred part of existence, by a cessation, the waiting and the momentary suicide. The knowledge which would become resplendent – of a pride attached to their daily work, to resist, simply and appear standing tall – is round about magnified by a colonnade of full-grown trees; some instinct sought it in a considerable number, to twist them thus about, of drinks, and they are from them, with the absoluteness of a ritual consummation, less officiants than victims, occupied in representing, in the evening, the stupefaction of tasks if the observance derives from fatality rather than a will.

The constellations are beginning to shine; how I would wish that within the darkness which falls over the blind herd, points of brightness also, a certain thought just now, should be fixed, despite these sealed eyes which do not distinguish them – for the fact, for exactness, in order that it may be said. I shall, therefore, think of them alone, the intruders, who, by their surrender more than erstwhile by their turmoil, are closing off from me the distant twilight. These artisans of elementary tasks, it is permissible to me, watching over them near a limpid continuous river, to see in them the people – a healthy understanding of the human condition bends their back daily in order to draw, without the intermediary of wheat, the miracle of life which assures presence: others have made past land-clearings and aqueducts or will submit a strip of land to such and such a machine, the same, Louis-Pierre, Martin, Poitou and the Norman, thus they call each other, when they don't sleep, according to their mothers or their province; but births sank rather into anonymity, and the immense sleep with their ear to mother earth, exhausting them, this time, undergoes an overwhelming and an enlargement of all the ages and, as much as that is possible – reduced to social proportions, of eternity.

At first, Mallarmé admits his preference for self-sufficiency; this piece will celebrate its breakdown. But we must be careful to note that transcendence can occur in this direction. There was no lack of self-surpassing in him vertically, in poetic vision and thought, creativity. But here he "adds" (though "multiply" is closer to the intimate process) the horizontal dimension of going beyond, which rounds out his creative universe in a fashion germane to the prose poem generically. He is not Leo Tolstoy – with his "génie simple et ample" as he put it in an interview[5] – but none the less he is, in this, closer to that secret Russian brother-under-the-skin than one might think: the haying scene in *Anna Karenina* provides a clue to the affinity.

He had thought, over a long period, that his "idée," his literary vision, would remain uncluttered by random reality, accidents. But he now has to change his view ("se dédire") as a result of his return to his summer residence.

raccorder: ambiguously, link the shutter to the wall, his glance to the scene, himself to the new reality.

Mallarmé rehearses in memory his earlier awareness, through rumor ("légende") of the threatened invasion, his consequent hesitation about leaving Paris, his final determination to defend the "insulted" heaven: so here he was.

The worn state of the corduroy on the laborers' legs indicates work done, progress on the railway embankment. The syntax is fluid: "par qui" can link the workers directly to "semble" – "the workers through whom the enbankment moves" or "through whom the worn corduroy seems like moving earth," just as their blue-and-white striped jerseys are like water (that their digging would cause to well up).

He reflects that man's outer clothes, in this case, symbolize the inner source (psychic "water") he is seeking. That interior water is, we recall, an image of *Le Nénuphar blanc*; the theme of reciprocity between man and his origin is widespread in Mallarmé: music, for example, is what joins mankind to itself as totality, its over-soul, "l'instinct de ciel en chacun." This is the nub of the word "hymn" as he uses it in the notes Bonniot published with *Igitur*, and generally.

choyés: this indicates a sort of envy of their romanticized freedom (in his mind). In this sense "quelconque" expresses their enviable independence of "usines" (later). These are itinerant workers, *chemineaux* with some of the cachet accorded gypsies or bohemians,[6] wandering poets (*cf. Le Guignon*) or players (Gautier's *Capitaine Fracasse*).

les maîtres si quelque part: wherever they settle to work, they dominate, through sheer brute presence, noise, etc. The *Maître* of the *Coup de Dés* is a hardy ancestor of this sort as we saw him in our study of the poem; see below.

This crowd forces one – since direct action is blocked by their superior physical strength, their implacable presence – to draw on hidden emotions ("derrière la tête") and literary ideas. This ambivalent mood, involving a sublimation of anger (as in the Oedipal crisis described by Freud and Lacan), characterizes his "religious" awe at seeing the tools lined up in the dwelling's basement. This religiosity, based on his filial respect for ancient striving, is, to repeat, in addition to his "mécontentement." Mallarmé kept his sailboats in that basement: he was the (sailing) *Maître* too, in his basement–psyche, as well as the upstairs poet (a spiral staircase joined that upper and lower self). This is all worked out beautifully in the *Coup de Dés*.[7]

The dialectical doubleness is also in his relation to the tools: Mallarmé is of a superior class, but they and their wielders impress him with their universality, going back in prehistory to organic sexual forms, male and female (pick and shovel), and are parts of the prestige of prior simplicity, immemorial ancestral forms and people like the workers. Again, I think of that bear and all the other animals representing archetypal motifs which combine schematically to give main strands of evolution, in fragments of *Le Livre*.[8] In *L'Œuvre de Mallarmé*, I demonstrate the parallel relation in the *Coup de Dés* between the hardy ancestor, *le Maître*, and his finer heir, the *ombre puérile* leading to a Hamlet figure and eventually the ultimate poet.

The ambivalence is expressed in the words "force" and "pure," which Mallarmé usually reserves for his "turf," art; here it is aggressively–affectionately – fecundly – applied to the energies of simple strong men doing things, instrumentally, to the original turf.

The word "résumant" is comparably prestigious for Mallarmé; it plays a prominent role, for example, on page 3 of the *Coup de Dés*, where elemental forces are being crystallized, condensed, "puckered" and *aufgehoben*, as they are in sexual commerce and they will be in the analogous act of the artist, later. The series of *u*'s in the sentence probably has to do with this intimate process (see Chapter 1, on *Le Démon de l'Analogie*.)

Aucun homme de loi: by local usage, and/or writ, etc., the law cannot do anything about this encroachment. Mallarmé sees that he himself will have to take care of his rights. He imagines himself addressing the men to that democratic end and refuses to alter his high style with "promiscuity, unlike others, these days" ("couramment"). Can he harangue, as he then queries, in precise ("juste") Mallarméan manner? Of course, he is aware of the humor in this proposition. But he feels they wouldn't laugh at him (unlike some bourgeois neighbors; why he suggests "eleven" I have no idea). He surmises that as drunkards they have some sense of the marvelous (art) and as hard workers, some notion of superior difficulties. In "délicatesses" there is a hint too of something fine glimmering at the end, like Eden for toiling Adam.

This high–low communion, skimping on the middling (middle-class, neighbors) is typical of elevated vision: Proust similarly remarks the kinship in accent between the Duchesse de Guermantes and her peasants, *versus* the mediocre Verdurins. Because of this meeting of extremes, the workers would see any differences as personal – sideways – and not one of class, vertically. They would look at each other a bit, then go back to whatever they were doing (and not laugh); unless one of them answered equably and explained their loudness. Mallarmé's imagining here is implausible and he knows it. It is just to dramatize his sympathetic meditations about what makes them the way they are. Since he now understands them, he lets down his defenses and invites the "attacker" into the sacred-to-the-bourgeois Property, which he capitalizes with bombastic irony. He has on purpose refrained from buying it (he just rents) out of the previously-mentioned instinct of artistic *dégagement*, as a mere "passant" – a term he favored in fully existential poems such as the *Toast funèbre*, applied to Gautier, who had little to do with a religious Home or Property.

selon que je me fis: implies Mallarmé's spiritual maturation (*se faire*: to ripen) in this deep encounter with proletarians. But let us keep our perspective; this is not the humorless Sartre at the gate of Citroën; there is no "camarade Mallarmé," *pace* the quondam *Tel Quellistes* . . .

Alternatives: He foresees the mixed mood of the newly-discovered sympathy along with the distaste, an uneasy hesitation altogether.

He considers cutting through the oscillation by a direct quarrel with a worker, man to man. Meanwhile, the only possible strategy is to lock the garden gate and force the workers to take a new path, cutting through the nearby planted field, to the canteen.

One drunk worker does assail him verbally through that shut gate, kicking it. But Mallarmé refuses to look down on him, and understands his resentment.

He showed his compassion for the underdog in various writings: in his defense of old beleaguered Ferdinand de Lesseps ("Or"), and persecuted anarchists ("Laurent Tailhade"); in conversation with Théodore Nathanson he worried about Dreyfus.[9] Fragments of *Pour un Tombeau d'Anatole* show that he occasionally thought of his son as a potential victim of relative poverty, with a certain momentary bitterness having to do with the child's sickness and death. But usually he was centrist, with (like Proust) a certain stake in elite society (they shared acquaintance with le Comte de Montes-quiou) as well as the other pole; basically he was *au-dessus de la mêlée* (or *en-dessous*) as most great artists really are; we saw that as being his complex position in *Pauvre Enfant pâle*.

Here he keeps quiet before the aggression, ruminating that there is no point in riposting verbally or otherwise: drink, it is implied, born of social frustration, is bringing this fellow low in place of any action by the poet–resident. And he sadly reflects that just in keeping silent he is somehow guilty of complicity in a class oppression. This conflict, echoed in the title, is felt to be a sort of drunken malaise rubbed off from the worker's degraded condition, which implies, once again, a deep compassion.

The calm which he habitually experiences in a rural region where noise would echo in the silence – and maybe the place was conducive to echoes generally – and particularly on Sunday even-ings, seems to prolong the *mutisme* he felt guilty about, in his non-response. The "apprehension" refers to a possible worry about external conflict with the workers, as an unsure hour descends symbolically in a daily *crise*, which he likes to have someone bear witness to. The *crise* is also his inner one, of course, his *conflit*. The "someone" is a bit vague – it probably refers ahead to the workers who also appreciate the moment – but in any case it relates the "tragedy of nature" to human times of day or year, as is clearly implied in the program for a Great Work:

quelque recours très simple et primitif, par exemple la symphonique équation propre aux saisons, habitude de rayon et de nuée; deux remar-ques ou trois d'ordre analogue à ces ardeurs, à ces intempéries par où notre passion relève des divers ciels . . .   (*La Musique et les Lettres*, p. 646)

So the essential meaning is that his meditation on men's (social and other) conflicts is rooted in cosmic forces, such as the (paired, sexually dialectical) tools were. Man's conflicts and nature's *crises* are in a tetrapolar relation, and the man–nature polarity brings this to polypolarity. In this same way, a sexual polarity and a physical concave–convex polarity (the receptacle and aggressive spike of *pelle* and *pioche*) form another tetrapolarity with a further cognate tension in the opposition of tools and nature, creating another polypolar nexus.[10] The whole text is a tissue of such complexities.

The workers seem to concur in his sense of a special hour, and argue, in their version of *crise*. Mallarmé can neither leave them nor join them fully – he is suspended at his window; and again, we see the importance of this image to the prose poem generically, this *crossing* place (*croisée*) between indoors and out, up and down, them and me, nature and civilization.

Sometimes, he sighs, there is no contact among men. He will make one of his own sort, out of his frustration. He imagines their opposition to him in phrases expressing their resentment at having to work so hard to build railways for the bourgeois, and he cooks up inwardly a response that the railway was not for him. This kind of dialogue, frequent in reality, is held in by his muteness and restraint; it is fortunately not heard in this enchanted setting of a spring evening. The stars are coming out, as "vain" as his art is to them – and to mankind generally, he often noted: *vide* the *désuétude* of the constellation. They stand, partly, for his rarefied expression at the end of the *Coup de Dés*.[11] The workers would understand (because of accountants, and the like) mental work, but not his kind, he sadly suspects.

The workers have fallen in a drunken stupor, as on a battlefield. The poet's vision of the horizon is interrupted by them – he can't get over them, literally and figuratively. This is the budding dimension of *engagement* of his special sort.

Again, he sees them as above (below) the mediocre, since their drunken quest for Something goes beyond daily bread.[12]

The *jonchée* – bodies scattered on the field – must be understood by him.

la voici: here that *jonchée* is: "tomorrow" does not exist for them; they are "picking" in their dreams (*vague*), motionless, and this makes in their destiny a "hole" – a rest, a vacancy, as in "vacation" – like the ones they dig in their daytime labors. The allusion to temple foundations refers ambiguously to their real work and the ideality of their inner "dreamwork" (Freud).

This hole has counterparts in various texts. It is the hunger hole of expectation, exactly analogous to an empty stomach, or pit,[13] e.g. "le gouffre de vaine faim" (p. 298) which is humanity's hopes for true art, dashed as usual in his time; the *attente* of *Toast funèbre* is parallel, betokening, as here, a sort of universal waiting for Godot (*cf.* the divine *sitio*). They celebrate this hunger or thirst for Edenic totality – "la part du sacré" – in their own way, unconsciously, as the *pauvres* of Baudelaire's *Le Vin* had movingly done. Their knowledge of this transcendence is sought instinctively in a considerable number of glasses of wine; the transcendence is in the human dignity of raising up works, standing up (*debout*)[14] in honest striving, and is reflected in the natural dignity of tall Fontainebleau forest trees all around; one recalls that paradigm from *La Gloire*. Their ritual is passively observed, by them as victims (Mallarmé is the conscious officiator) brought low by hard labor; it is seen in the light of fatality, eternity, as opposed to ordinary human will to build.

The stars coming out confirm this cosmic scenario (note the series of *i*'s for brilliance). Mallarmé wants his own clarity of thought to imitate them out of a sort of cosmic clarity in the form of his disinterested art. They are all unknowing, of course, but he is their fraternal spokesman. They perform as their ancestors did the basic tasks of living for all men: clearing ground, building aqueducts. Their sobriquets often reveal their mother-provinces – Poitou, Normandy – but their truest mother, on which they are lying, is the Magna Mater of us all, earth. As much as possible, given the real proportions of the social beings here and now, they are part of the everlasting.

They are undergoing a sort of baptism of *accablement*, humble as Saint John is said to be in the *Noces*,[15] hungry too in their way, dying to live beyond, to be reborn to all.

So ends, rather solemnly, the thirteenth prose poem and the collection. Can we read any significance into this number? The *Atelier/Change* group of critics, who produced a fine edition of the *Coup de Dés*, thought everything in Mallarmé was based on the number twelve. I tried to show the obvious limitation of this view in a little note in the review *Critique*.[16] Mallarmé liked all sorts of numbers, it is easy to prove. Thirteen, a baker's dozen, does not seem to attract him in any particular way that I am aware of. Does it start a new cycle, as in Nerval's "La Treizième revient"? Twelve would seem a better symbol of a cycle, the hours and months typically, and Mallarmé does favor that occasionally, we know.

Maybe there is something to the idea of baker's dozen, a breaking out of the patness of symmetry in a vibrant way – even and odd both, suggestively.

CONCLUSION

The prevailing image that emerges in retrospect from these pieces is that of a central figure, the artist himself, encountering a variety of reality, more or less fascinating poetically, in a setting that is often identifiable as his home city, Paris, in the late nineteenth century; or nearby places such as London, Valvins and the provinces.

There are theorists in our time, such as Roman Ingarden, who are quick to object that the writer himself, as a person, has nothing to do with texts like these. Well, Mallarmé's poetic universe, the *Jeu suprême*, was made up of sparkling paradoxical play in all directions, and the author–text relation is one of these, certainly in works like the prose poems which he himself characterized as anecdotal. Let us say that, given the fundamental vibrancy of his reality – which he called "fiction" on occasion or "artifice" in one of our texts, *Un Spectacle interrompu* – the central figure is in the same situation as Kafka's K. or Proust's Marcel, both the author and not ... We can call our discreet hero M. or Stéphane in this elusive sense.

We see our gentle Stéphane moving around the city, puzzled by an eerie *déjà vu* in a shop window near his apartment (rue de Rome, dare I add), going to an unexpectedly wild performance at a popular theater, witnessing a bizarre private exhibition in the Bois de Boulogne, taking his buxom lady friend to a vulgar fair. He listens to a pale child singing for his life in a Parisian street, or a nostalgic barrel-organ which reminds him of the death of his sister in autumn. He takes us back, for a spell, to anxious earlier days as a lonely child, as a young newly-wed waiting for news from his absent wife, later in a provincial town with her in dreamy winter domesticity. Or he glances forward at a time when the decadence he feels growing around him will have obliterated the natural beauty of woman. Finally, he takes a train to escape that pall of modern civilization and finds relief, true glory, in the autumn woods of Fontainebleau, near his villa at Valvins; there, he rows up a branch of the Seine one impressionistic summer day and encounters an invisible lady whom he guesses to be hidden amid the foliage of her estate: this is the exquisite presence–absence we associate particularly with Mallarmé. In the villa itself, he has a profound *encounter* (in the Buber sense) with his fellow-man – railway workers – for whom he feels a vast sympathy, under the eternal stars.

Those are the settings and the events, *grosso modo*, but what we retain most of all is an intimate late-Romantic temperament gingerly experiencing a world that is as mysterious as it is present, vivacious, and varied; a lonely modern psyche, almost too sensitive to live but going on anyway with what Joyce called "timid courage," rewarded now and then by privileged moments including an almost Tolstoyan love of life. One readily thinks of Malte Laurids Brigge or his creator, Rilke – should we say R.? – idling curiously along those same Parisian streets, remembering no doubt his admired predecessors, Baudelaire and Mallarmé, who had stumbled over those cobblestones "dans la rue/Et dans le soir . . . "

Or we can think of Apollinaire, Fargue, Picasso, Eluard, just as gratefully and movingly remembering, at many a familiar corner of their itineraries. What we are talking about here is, after all, a whole artistic era that is the wider aura surrounding and to a considerable extent emerging quite directly from these choice pages, however *oubliées*.

NOTES

Introduction

1 In *The Prose Poem in France*, edited by Mary Ann Caws and Hermine Riffaterre (New York: Columbia University Press, 1983), pp. 135–62.
2 This aspect of Mallarmé's universe is treated in my "Urban Mallarmé", in *Stanford French Review*, 9:1 (1985), 61–9.
3 In *Le Dernier Baudelaire* (Paris: Corti, 1966).
4 "Baudelaire's Beleaguered Prose Poems," in *Textual Analysis*, edited by Mary Ann Caws, The Modern Language Association of America (New York, 1986).
5 In the final publication as part of *Divagations*, in 1897 (Charpentier) under the title *Anecdotes ou Poëmes*. Previously the thirteen pieces had appeared in various reviews, starting in 1864. The first twelve were provisionally gathered together in 1891 in the selection of his work called *Pages* (Deman, Bruxelles).
6 *An Anatomy of Poesis: The Prose Poems of Stéphane Mallarmé*, North Carolina Studies in the Romance Languages and Literature, No. 16 (Chapel Hill, 1976).

1 Le Démon de l'Analogie

1 North Carolina Studies in the Romance Languages and Literature, No. 16 (Chapel Hill, 1976).
2 Plain numbers refer to the Gallimard (NRF) edition of the *Œuvres complètes*.
3 (Paris: Ollendorf, 1931), p. 116.
4 See my *L'Œuvre de Mallarmé: Un Coup de Dés* (Paris: Librairie Les Lettres, 1951), and *Toward the Poems of Mallarmé*, paperback edition (Berkeley: University of California Press, 1981).
5 See *Toward the Poems of Mallarmé*, pp. 263–4.
6 This "ideal–sensual" fusion is *par excellence* poetic, vertical; the combination probably associated with a hidden memory of his sister is found in an early poem, *Læda*; compare the women–swans of *Faune* in our study of the latter in *Toward the Poems of Mallarmé*.
7 In *L'Œuvre de Mallarmé*, Mallarmé's anagrammatical technique was

explored extensively. In his *Mallarmé* (Editora da Universidade de Saô Paulo, 1975), Augusto de Campos remarks that this investigation "precedes the work of Starobinski on the manuscripts of Saussure" (p. 121, my translation).

8 This theme is treated in my "O quel lointain: Memory in Mallarmé," *Romanic Review*, 70:2 (March 1979), 133–45.

9 See Vol. 1 of the *Correspondance* (Paris: Gallimard, 1959), letter to Cazalis of 30 January 1983 (pp. 73–5). At an extremity, underneath, there is at least a suggestion of the divine Mary. Surely woman is a complex entity, polypolar (bipolar, tetrapolar, etc.). The Oedipal triangle of Freud tends to hypostatize woman in a fixed entity. She is far more fleeting: she is above all mother–daughter; she is saint–witch, mother–sister, Berthe–Ondine, etc. All these pairs of (paradoxically interpenetrating) ambiguous poles form dimensions which in turn interpenetrate and cross each other in a *chassé-croisé* or polypolar game.

In general, triangulation limits thought whereas the polypolar opens it. Thus it is better to envisage play between two women (mother–daughter) and two men (father–son), at least in the Oedipal merry-go-round. The *Elective Affinities* of Goethe illustrates this evidence. There, again, the two dimensions, masculine and feminine, cross each other, given, for Goethe and true life, the relatively horizontal status of femininity – "concatenation," as he says in the novel; compare the eternal feminine which pulls us along (*hinan*), the primary aspect of this term having been badly translated and misunderstood. But, of course, this criss-cross is also interpenetration; the feminine often pivots to a vertical transcendance in the true game of existence, the "Icarian" male toils Adamically, etc.

This same complexity defines desire. It is a play of dimensions: adorations (metaphorical, integral, paradoxical) and ordinary desires (metonymic, partial, univocal) which cross each other and interprenetrate one another (and even can be identical) in the long run (or in depth). One must point out, despite Lacan and Girard, that *adoration* (much more omnipresent, intermittent, than they think) is not *need* (animal), but it also *is*, at the same time! This is the vibrant fuller truth on the metaphorical dimension (*cf.* our sky–milk, erotic religion, Plato's sacred–profane in *The Symposium*, etc.). The great literary texts affirm this, an example being "the perpetual Adoration" of Proust. "Perpetual Imitation" also exists, agreed, since *la vraie vie* is made up of plural infinites. But why the monotonous *reduction* to this one dimension? Imitation is limitation. Narration without the sacred, the visionary, the poetical, the paradigmatical, quality, or values, is a mutilation of life.

10 Derrida, incidentally, made a particular point of defending my chain of *analogies* involving the feather against Jean-Pierre Richard's curiously crusty strictures; see *La Dissémination*, pp. 305–6.

11 See *L'Œuvre de Mallarmé*, p. 144, where I give these further examples: "elles se confondirent ... le battement d'ailes" (*Igitur*, 437) and "séraphins ailés des cieux convoitaient à elle" (p. 202).

12 There is a corollary dialectic in the *p versus* the *m* of *plume*; also the brightness of overtones like *lumière*, *écume* and the softness of feathers and, again, the *m*, which is very much involved in the closing lines of the *Ouverture ancienne d'Hérodiade*, featuring the feminine aspect of the swan feathers.

13 See for example "On the Sexual Theories of Children" (1908), and, in particular, "Some Psychological Consequences of the Anatomical Distinction between the Sexes" (1925).

14 See *L'Œuvre de Mallarmé*, pp. 133–4.

15 *Mallarmé: Igitur* (Berkeley: University of California Press, 1981), pp. 26–32.

16 See *Toward the Poems of Mallarmé*, pp. 23–4.

17 The overtone of *sein–saint* may well have something to do with the Saint Jean decapitation and white Eros (*lait*) spurting up which we discussed earlier; see *Toward the Poems of Mallarmé*, p. 88. The shift from breast to male expression (sexual) is very deliberately portrayed in Imamura's *The Ballad of Narayama*.

18 Banville was a major influence on Mallarmé in this respect. Orpheus is an important figure in his ambitious poem, *La Voie lactée*; it certainly had an impact on the complex dialectic of artistic becoming in the *Coup de Dés*. See *L'Œuvre de Mallarmé*, p. 239, footnote 54.

19 Barbara Johnson's deconstructive critique (in *Défigurations du langage poétique* (Paris: Flammarion, 1979)) of this text seems to me to be incorrect in her assumption that the penult refers to a last-but-one rhyme which dies in thin air, since, from this viewpoint, there is no real rhyme in life; hence, the argument goes, Mallarmé was already burning what he had adored, poetry, and on the way to a mixed prose–poetry as here and in the *Coup de Dés*, along with his whole century. But a rhyme is part of a *couple*, not a penult in a *series*. Besides Mallarmé was not at all giving up on verse poetry at this point. He always regarded these prose poems as "Anecdotes" and "Pages oubliées," i.e. very apologetically (*cf.* the title *Divagations*, where they finally appeared together). Granted that he had some fertile doubts about poetry which showed up in his critical ruminations later, it seems clear that many modern critics exaggerate everything in this direction for their obsessive purposes and that at most, given the full poetic and imaginative metapsychological charge of the term *Pénultième* properly understood, this is one very minor possibility among many. The idea offered by other critics that the *Pénultième* would be a one-before-the-last woman to die (his mother before his sister) seems to me too awkward and programmatic. As far as I know, Mallarmé never expressed himself in this fashion.

20 In *Remémoration des amis belges*, the spiraled cycles of the different

levels of the *Souvenir* are presented: total time *à la* Plato (*Meno*: re-incarnation, etc.), youth or golden age of the tradition, personal childhood, and so on; see my "O quel lointain," cited above.

21 Henri de Régnier, *Nos rencontres* (Mercure de France, 1931), p. 192. See also my review of Austin Gill's *The Early Mallarmé* in *Romanic Review*, 74:1 (1983), 108–9; Gill, in my view, very wrongly slights the importance for the poet of this powerful inner event.

22 Thus Simone de Beauvoir, for instance, makes a mistake in insisting on the quality "other" of the "second" sex. It is evident that it is man who is "other," a mental reservation of the creation. Abstraction, and the desire to fly, are an imperious necessity for him. See my "On Human Gender" in *Modes of Art* (Saratoga, California: Anima Libri, 1975).

23 This has been discussed in my "From Chrétien to Camus: Plumes and Prisons," Appendix C of *Ways of Art*, Stanford French and Italian Studies (Saratoga, California, 1985).

24 This explains the well-known anthropological phenomenon of the "couvade," a man trying to imitate his wife giving birth. Karen Horney and Lillian Rubin are among the psychologists who speak of "womb envy," which, although more subtle than the jealousy of the penis – because of the *absence* which is envied; this absence–totality that man must seek in his own soul – is far more important. Note that the principle of spirit, rather masculine, is equally profoundly rooted in the cosmos and epistemology; it is on this earth that the primacy and the centrality of woman is exerted ... this common earth, between "heaven" and "hell," therefore relatively horizontal in the great dimensional game.

25 One thinks of "the simple insinuation" which initiates the development of the artistic becoming in the *Coup de Dés*; the embryonic rhythm which sets off the poetic expression of Valéry; and a thousand other examples.

26 A few details:

"le doigt sur l'artifice du mystère": that fine finger is typical of Mallarmé's gingerliness and modesty or discretion; the image is ubiquitous in his work. The "délicate phalange" of *Sainte* is near to this finger, involved similarly with wings and musical instruments.

"la phrase revint, virtuelle": being "dégagée," as he says, from the "plume" and "rameau," it has an original purity and independence, and may be ready to say something on its own, hence "virtuelle," pregnant with promise.

"psalmodie": another *mot–carrefour*, connecting with *palmes*, which in turn link up with his oriental princess, Hérodiade, on whom he was working around this time. Hence too the nearby *psaume*, as in the fragment of *Hérodiade* beginning "A quel psaume de nul antique."

2 Le Phénomène futur

1 See my *The Writer's Way in France* (Philadelphia: University of Pennsylvania Press, 1960), pp. 192–3, where I treat this phenomenon of phenomenality in Rousseau, Nerval, Mallarmé.

2 In *Mallarmé chez lui*, Camille Mauclair (Paris: Grasset, 1935), p. 117.

3   Un jeune écrivain a eu récemment une conception ingénieuse, mais non absolument juste. Le monde va finir. L'humanité est décrépite. Un Barnum de l'avenir montre aux hommes dégradés de son temps une belle femme des anciens âges artificiellement conservée. "Eh quoi! disent-ils, l'humanité a-t-elle pu être aussi belle que cela." Je dis que cela n'est pas vrai. *L'homme dégradé s'admirerait et appellerait la beauté la laideur.*

(cited by Mondor, *Correspondance de Mallarmé*, Vol. 1, p. 201, and Ursula Franklin, *op. cit.*)

4 Predecessors are Baudelaire's *Vieux saltimbanque*, Poe's "literary histrion" in *The Poetic Principle*, Banville's *Le Tremplin*.

5 *Cf.* "le vieux mal de vivre" in *Pour un Tombeau d'Anatole*. The "péché des siècles" in *active* evil, sin (not specified) – *cf.* "le démon immémorial," *Coup de Dés*, page 5 – and "la maladie immortelle" a passive entity, the germ of death in all, *ab ovo*, as on page 3 of the *Coup de Dés*: "par avance . . . mal."

6 I discuss this in *Modes of Art* under "On Human Gender," citing Karen Horney's "womb envy" and anthropological data.

7 This dialectic of dimensions is the core of Mallarméan vision, as in the "équation symphonique propre aux saisons" (*La Musique et les Lettres*). I call this "polypolarity" (including "tetrapolarity", etc.). See my *L'Œuvre de Mallarmé*, under *Syntax*.

8 *Cf.* Goethe's *Ewig-Weibliche* in *Faust* and woman as central "linkage" in time in *The Elective Affinities*. See also Camus' mother-figure in *La Peste*.

9 This is treated extensively in my discussion of *Prose* (*pour des Esseintes*) in *Toward the Poems of Mallarmé*, pp. 257–60.

10 This "tragedy of nature" theme will be discussed under *Plainte d'automne*.

11 In his *Baudelaire and Freud* (University of California Press, 1977), Leo Bersani sees Baudelaire's image as *replacing* the real woman, who is not so interesting. This is a veritable crusade on his part. But who does not use a part to "get a handle" on forbidding wholes? This is a general human phenomenon. Nothing indicates that Baudelaire did not *also* go beyond the "fetich."

12 These poetic clusters, which Mallarmé alludes to in a famous passage ("Les mots s'exaltent," etc., in "Le Mystère dans les lettres," p. 386) are discussed in my *L'Œuvre de Mallarmé*, pp. 91–3, and throughout *Toward the Poems of Mallarmé*.

13 Dr René Laforgue studies this motif in *L'Echec de Baudelaire* (Paris: Denoël et Steele, 1931).

14 I show this effect in twin window-curtains in *Modes of Art, op. cit.* p. 61. *Une dentelle s'abolit*, as I study it in *Toward the Poems of Mallarmé*, the two-in-one paradox of gender, *pli*, etc., is also seen in the reverse aspect of duality as female moving toward male unity.

15 Outlined in various of my books: *Modes of Art, Mallarmé: Igitur* (University of California Press, 1981); *L'Œuvre de Mallarmé*.

3 Plainte d'automne

1 Austin Gill in *The Early Mallarmé* (Oxford: OUP, 1979) dismisses this as sentimental solicitation of texts. I differ with him in my review of his books, in *Romanic Review*, 74:1 (1983), 108–9.

2 This umbilical cord of tradition is a temporal version of "l'omni-présente Ligne" *(La Musique et les Lettres)*.

3 Léon Cellier, in *Mallarmé et la Morte qui parle* (Paris: Presses Universi-taires de France, 1959), gives book-length attention to this motif, excellently. Mann prolongs it in his short story, *The Blood of the Walsungs*.

Death is easily entangled with incest-dread and fascination. In Debussy's unfinished opera, *La Chute de la Maison Usher*, the emotion got too deep and he could not go on. What we have, now recorded, is blood-curdling.

4 In *Documents Stéphane Mallarmé* (Paris: Nizet, 1968), pp. 9 ff.

5 See my Letter Table, under *a*, in *Toward the Poems of Mallarmé*.

4 Frisson d'hiver

1 Aloysius Bertrand had used this incantatory device often. I demon-strate a similar use of four entities in a number of Baudelaire's prose poems ("Baudelaire's Beleaguered Prose Poems," in *Textual Approaches*).

2 George Moore, in *Avowals*, (New York: Boni and Liveright, 1919), pp. 276–81, reports a Mallarméan project involving an indoor–outdoor opposition of this sort: the wind howls, and if it rises, making an *ou* sound into *oui*, the protagonist will depart from his solitary castle.

3 This basic structure of poetry is discussed in *Modes of Art*, p. 60.

4 Compare Baudelaire's remarks on rigging in motion (*Journal intime*; also "Le Peintre de la vie moderne").

5 This static–dynamic pairing is treated in "Mallarmé's Poetic Vision," in *Toward the Poems of Mallarmé*. The mirror–fountain of *Hérodiade* is a prime example.

6 See the reference in note 5, where this core imagery is discussed *in extenso*.

7 One can suspect, as I have shown elsewhere (*Toward the Poems of*

Mallarmé, p. 59) a forbidden incestuous glimpse of the beloved dead sister or mother; compare the dreamed-of *blasphème*, violation of the divine Venus, in the *Faune*.

8 Malraux, in *La Condition humaine*, has Valérie muse about this.

9 See the Letter Table in *Toward the Poems of Mallarmé*.

10 This is discussed in my *The Poetry of Rimbaud* (Princeton University Press, 1973), under *Jeune Ménage*.

11 See the reference in note 5.

12 Discussed in *Toward the Poems of Mallarmé*.

13 " . . . elle est mon enfant" (*Correspondance*, Vol. 1, p. 70); "Pauvre petite enfant" (p. 71).

5 Pauvre Enfant pâle

1 See Appendix A in *Toward the Poems of Mallarmé*.

2 See under *Le Cantique de Saint Jean*.

3 See under *p* in the *Letter Table*.

4 See *L'Œuvre de Mallarmé*, pp. 133–4ff. Also *Mallarmé: Igitur* (University of California Press, 1981), pp. 27–30.

5 See *Toward the Poems of Mallarmé*, under *Hérodiade*, p. 53.

6 This motif is studied in Appendix C: "Plumes and Prisons" in *Ways of Art* (Saratoga, California: Anma Libri, 1985).

7 See under *t* in the *Letter Table*.

6 La Pipe

1 See *Modes of Art*, p. 59.

2 See my "Proust and Mallarmé" in *French Studies*, 24:3 (1970), 262–75.

3 See *Toward the Poems of Mallarmé*, pp. 129–30.

4 This preceding paragraph is taken from my "A Poetry Prose Cross", p. 155.

5 She is an Other only fugitively, or slightly (as in the reminiscence of her far-away provenance and, at the end, "Tu es distraite?"). But that is always potential, as in any movement from *tu* to *vous* (as in Racine *et al.*). So she contributes little to the Otherness implied in prose: mainly she is a co-subjectivity (*tu*). It is the outdoors which is the Other, suggesting the final Other, death, the ocean–water of *La Pipe*.

6 See the letter to Cazalis (*Correspondance*, Vol. 1, pp. 73–5) where he links his duty to Marie with his dead mother and sister, "up there." I comment on this in "Plumes and Prisons."

7 Cigarettes seem frivolous, in this sense – part of the less-adult phase. The theme of childhood transparency is prominent in *Las de l'amer repos*.

8 Pissarro paints vivid and grimy smoking steamers, e.g. at Rouen, which could illustrate this passage ideally.

9 In *La Peste*; also a more detailed account of her published separately as a story. Baudelaire indulged this mood of attractive poverty in pieces like *Les Petites vieilles*, *La Vieille*; Rimbaud in *Les Pauvres à l'église*.

10 In *Brise marine* it joins with seabirds and foam; in "adieu suprême des mouchoirs" the white beauty (with erotic undertones) links with death; see *Toward the Poems of Mallarmé* under *Brise marine*.

7 Un Spectacle interrompu

1 Of course, Shakespeare had struck the same provocative posture with his "We are such stuff as dreams are made on" and so had the Baroque era generally, with, for example, Calderon's *Life is a Dream*. And, much earlier, there were Plato and Plutarch . . .

2 "Martin" is a stock name for show bears in France. "Atta Troll" is Heine's name for a bear in a famous satirical poem.

3 The two and multiple nymphs of the *Faune* are a rough equivalent of this. In *Le Livre* a metaphysical protagonist is flanked by two troupes of women.

4 Compare the *dénégation* imitated by the panache floating over the non-nuptial bed of *Hérodiade* (*Noces*, p. 60).

5 *L'Ecclésiastique* ends on just this note, which goes back to Gautier's "le buste survit à la cité," and Renaissance themes, in Ronsard for example. Mallarmé's "Ces nymphes je les veux perpétuer" will subtly prolong this line.

6 "Sans que m'offusquât l'attitude probablement fatale prise par le mime dépositaire de notre orgueil": this indicates that Mallarmé will ignore the (probably inevitable) horror in the clown as he has the bear utter his gravely calm speech.

7 It is a penetrating symbol of modernity for Mallarmé, here as in the *Tombeau de Charles Baudelaire* and various references in the essays on theater, and in *La Dernière Mode*.

8 An artist easily associates with a victim, and, more completely, tries to "touch all the bases" of reality in the wholeness of his vision; a good novelist, in that sense, is all his characters, as Camus observes.

9 Leconte de Lisle's elephants and condors illustrate the point.

10 He uses the term in this piece directly as well as for the collection as a whole.

8 Réminiscence

1 A Spanish psychiatrist named Ernesto Guarner had only matadors as his clientele; in a book studying them, he tells us that they were without exception fatherless.

2 In *Obliques*, Nos. 18 and 19, pp. 169–94.

3 This was pointed out to me by Nancy Ruttenberg, a graduate student at Stanford with X-ray eyes.

4 In his *Connaissance de Baudelaire* (Paris: Corti, 1951), p. 152.

9 La Déclaration foraine

1 This commentary is reprinted from *Toward the Poems of Mallarmé*.

2 That is obvious enough in many cases and there is no need to defend this view. Mallarmé at times, like men in all times including the present, asserts his male superiority, in part, no doubt, because of metapsychological vulnerability (compare discussion of this in my comment on *Don du Poème*, in *Toward the Poems of Mallarmé*). Baudelaire indulged this vein in his journals and prose poems, etc., but also apologized for it in "Le Peintre de la vie moderne" and a key passage of the journals involving total sympathy for a woman. Mallarmé honors the opposite sex in all sorts of ways, including an awed and honest homage to her natural creativity in *Don du Poème*. All told, he was quite balanced in this respect – very decent indeed to women and everybody else.

3 A close analogue is the "bark" of the train conductor ruining the mood of approaching Fontainebleau. In *Conflit* the poet confesses how hard he takes public noise.

4 Laughter for him is often, as for most of us, a spontaneous expression of on-going life and health in the face of some threat, such as an absurdity breaking down reason. That healthy aspect is evident here and a sign of his decency and wisdom despite his artist's distance from the crowd (*cf.* Tolstoy and the haymakers, or *Conflit* in this collection).

5 The *triomphe–trompette* echo is behind this image association, as in *Prose* and *Hommage à Richard Wagner*, *q.v.* in *Toward the Poems of Mallarmé*.

6 The stagnant also links up with the streaked dusk, marshy effect, as in *Autre éventail*: "nuages roses stagnant sur les soirs d'or."

7 In *Crise de vers* (p. 360) there is a reference to "une inquiétude de voile dans le temple," referring to the signs at the death of Christ and also of Hugo. Yeats used this idea in a title, *The Trembling Veil*.

8 Mallarmé uses this *lui–lui* echo in his essay on Rimbaud: "météore, lui!" Rimbaud himself does so in *Mémoire*, where the sun, his father, is *Lui*.

9 In notes on the theater Mallarmé decries "la prostitution en ce lieu" and "la chair pressée de dégorger cet éclair" (p. 322). Compare "La chair est triste, hélas" (*Brise marine*); he was no prude, but . . .

10 The clasping jewel is an attribute of Méry in various poems. See the appendix to *Le Nénuphar blanc*, where I demonstrate its deeply erotic character. See also the close of *Hérodiade, Scène*.

Chapter 9, Appendix

1 It is special in the work of Mallarmé inasmuch as it follows a Shakespearean sonnet form of three quatrains and a distich. No doubt for this

reason Mallarmé put it by itself, away from the other sonnets, in the edition of the *Poésies* which he was preparing when he died.

2 Perhaps like a comet (the root of "comet" is Greek *komé*, hair): "Je suis heureux, ravi de voir passer cette chevelure blonde dans ton ciel sans comète depuis longtemps" (in *L'Œuvre de Mallarmé*, p. 374).

3 The flare-up, a kinetic linear flight, gives way to the circular crown, a stasis; compare "ou traverse un tunnel ... avant la gare ... qui couronne" (371–2) and *L'Œuvre de Mallarmé*, p. 68.

4 Antoine Adam has proposed the reading "without sighing any gold except this live cloud" (the verb *continue* would be an indicative). This is a slight possibility; it is contradicted by the fact that the hair as cloud has now disappeared into a crown; moreover, this involves a strained and unprepossessing usage of *soupirer*.

5 "Et vos longs doigts, cinq rameaux inégaux,/Ne sont pompeux de bagues ni d'anneaux" (Ronsard, *Elégie à Marie Stuart*).

6 In all this Mallarmé is aiming at an art which will somehow not be alienated from but *be* life; at times, he thought the only way was to become impersonal – put "nothing" between the expression and the reality – by a sort of psychic suicide or total humility or anonymous invisibility: "anonyme et parfait ... art" (p. 367); "Mon théâtre [the world] de plain-pied et le fouler ... dans un congé de tous" (p. 403). See *L'Œuvre de Mallarmé*, p. 316. The *nue–nue* ambiguity is constant in Mallarmé; see *Quelle soie* and Gautier's *La Nue* (cloud–woman).

7 In this early unhappy poem (quoted under *Quelle soie* in my *Toward the Poems of Mallarmé*), however, the sparks of beauty brought Mallarmé back to a hated reality: "font naître/ D'atroces étincelles d'être/ Mon horreur et mes désaveux" (*Sonnet à Wyse*). The later poem expresses a more cheerful moment; perhaps Méry helped bring about this change of mood, as various commentators hold.

10 Le Nénuphar blanc

1 This absence–presence forms, together with the cognate ideal–sensual polarity, a tetrapolar "cross."

2 *Sainte* comes quickly to mind.

3 The vibrancy is, more complexly, polypolar, amid dialectical tensions of presence–absence, sensual–ideal, woman–flower (human–natural), etc.

4 The rose is a frequent symbol for woman in Mallarmé, in the *Faune*, *Hérodiade* ("la rose, cruelle," in *Les Fleurs*), many a sonnet to Méry and various juvenilia.

5 Commentators (including Raymond Bach) have seen this in connection with the quest for the lady in the park. This is likely. But there is no (crusty) allegory in Mallarmé: the "Hautaine, Méditative" etc. are not wooden allegorical masks of the lady but true live organic epithets, emanations of her into plural possible forms. The capitals add a note of discouraging generality, as we shall see.

6 This is a typically daring and effective ellipse, a synesthesia between aural and tactile. It is a part of the promiscuously harmonizing mood of the poem.

7 The repeated *v* is apt for this cleft in nature, as in "vallée." See the Letter Table in *Toward the Poems of Mallarmé*.

8 "Impartial" in the sense of not choosing any place to stop (so far).

9 The *parc* and *pelouses* have, of course, to do with the sexual undertone of the *inconnue* (*cf.* the biblical sense of "knowing"), as in Shakespeare's *Venus and Adonis*, Baudelaire's *La Géante*, Mallarmé's own erotic sonnet *M'introduire dans ton histoire*: "héros . . . s'il a du talon nu touché/Quelque gazon de territoire . . ." (the frequent *héros–Eros* echo in Mallarmé is noted in *Toward the Poems of Mallarmé*).

10 The universal analogy which links the watery mirror to woman's psychic essence, or *anima* (including fertility), is important in world literature and is present in Mallarmé, for example, in *Hérodiade, Ses purs ongles, Petit air II, Frisson d'hiver* . . .

11 See the Letter Table in *Toward the Poems of Mallarmé*.

12 See my comment on the first *coup* (and the overtone *coupe*) in my study of the *Coup de Dés*, p. 119–21.

13 See Appendix A in *Toward the Poems of Mallarmé*, pp. 261–2.

14 See the Epilogue of *Toward the Poems of Mallarmé*, where I discuss Mallarmé's windows.

Chapter 10, Appendix

1 The juxtaposition of *pense* and *conçoit* suggests a masculine–feminine ambiguity which is important in this part of the *Coup de Dés*.

2 This *site*, as in the *Coup de Dés*, signifies total circle or womb; the image of the diamond (clasp) is found in various poems to Méry; compare the *rejet* of *éternelles* on page 2, also "le palais de cette étrange bouche [vulve]" (*Une négresse*), and "le nid moussu d'un gai chardonneret" [sexe féminin] (*Mystacis umbraculis*). The "chardonneret," or finch, has red plumage.

3 *échappée*: "espace entre deux corps" (Larousse). We note, in passing, the *circonvenir* and *conduisent*, and, immediately following this passage, "Connaît-elle un motif à sa station?"

11 L'Ecclésiastique

1 The ambivalence here leads, perhaps, directly, to Eliot's "April is the cruellest month." Spring is often deadly, in fact, a favored time for suicide. The deep impulses well up and are hard to bear.

2 He wrote this in his article "L'Engagement de Mallarmé," published in *Obliques*, Nos. 18 and 19, pp. 169–94.

3 In *Les Premières communions*, Rimbaud focusses on the priestly shoes; man at his most transcendent still touches earth.

4 Stephen Dedalus, in *Portrait of the Artist*, saw the artist as an "androgynous angel." That is an old idea, much worked over in nineteenth-century literature (Balzac's *Seraphita* and *Sarrasine*, Gautier's *Mademoiselle de Maupin*, Baudelaire's *La Fanfarlo*, etc.).

5 In *La Gloire*: "l'ombre ici insinuée dans mon esprit" refers to dark suspicion released by a brutal event. In "Catholicisme", he refers to Greek tragedy as leaving a shiver in the "robes spectatrices" (as opposed to clear intellect) and hence "la terreur en ce pli" (p. 393). Dark mystery hovers in the folds of curtains in *Igitur, Les Noces d'Hérodiade*, etc. The play between cloth-folds, text-folds and brain folds occurs in the *Ouverture ancienne d'Hérodiade*:

> Encore dans les plis jaunes de la pensée
> ... Par les trous anciens et par les plis roidis
> Percés selon le rythme et les dentelles pures
> Du suaire laissant par ses belles guipures
> Désespéré monter le vieil éclat voilé

6 See *Toward the Poems of Mallarmé*, under these poem titles.

7 Greek *skéné*, "tent," was the origin of "scene."

12 La Gloire

1 Including the final apocalypse, this is the circle–line–circle (or globe–tube–globe) pattern of Eden and much else, e.g. of reproduction – from whole through genetic process to whole (heir), whether of persons or of model through articulatory process to artistic product. I allude to this "dumb-bell" shape in earlier studies of Mallarmé, who was very conscious of it. The horizontal "dumb-bell" is complemented by a vertical "hour-glass" (glory of related mind and genitals) in a tetrapolarity (*cf.* the four-globe *mandala*), which has as quintessential synthesis in a totalizing central Glory, of oversoul or eternal present, an instant of bliss ("privileged moment" "epiphany," etc.). See *Toward the Poems of Mallarmé, Epilogue*, p. 310, note 23.

2 For further comment, I refer the reader to my studies of the *Coup de Dés* (particularly page 7) and *Prose (pour des Esseintes)* in *Toward the Poems of Mallarmé*.

3 "Gloire" tended to mean this, i.e. "success" or "reputation," in the writings of the Classical era.

4 *Prose (pour des Esseintes)*. In my comment on this poem, in *Toward the Poems of Mallarmé*, I feature the phonostylistics which Mallarmé developed in *Les Mots anglais*, in connection with the letter *g*:

> G ... une aspiration simple ... le désir, comme satisfait par *l*, exprime avec la dite liquide, joie lumière, etc. (p. 938).

I added:

> An excellent example of the *gl* thus described is "Gloire du long désir" in *Prose* (p. 56); similarly, "sanglots glissants" (p. 30); "jailli le sanglot" (p. 66); "le cri des Gloires" (p. 76).

In a footnote I added further:

> With the word "gloire" is associated the word "glaïeul" and the form of the corolla, compare "blancs sanglots ... corolles" (p. 30) and "blancheur sanglotante des lys" (p. 34).

5 In *James Joyce* (Paris: La Hune, 1949), p. 5.

6 Among the examples I offer in my study of the *Coup de Dés*:

> tout à coup l'éruptif multiple sursautement de la clarté, comme les proches irradiations d'un lever de jour (p. 648)
>
> Hilare or de cymbales à des poings irrite/Tout à coup le soleil (p. 31)
>
> L'or de la trompette d'été (p. 56)
>
> Le vieil éclat . . ./ Jettera-t-il son or . . .? (p. 42)

And I add this:

> Dans "le Mystère dans les Lettres" (pp. 384–5) Mallarmé donne une indication frappante de son intention de commencer son Œuvre par la combinaison idée–dé–coup–éclat de soleil (premier coup d'une horloge astrale) heurt–heure–éclat triomphal de son été–âge d'or, etc.: "On peut, du reste, commencer d'un éclat triomphal trop brusque pour durer; invitant que se groupe, en retard, libérés par l'écho, la surprise.
>
> L'inverse: sont, en un reploiement noir soucieux d'attester l'état d'esprit sur un point, foulés et épaissis des doutes pour que sorte une splendeur définitive simple.
>
> Ce procédé, jumeau, intellectuel, notable dans les symphonies, qui le trouvèrent au répertoire de la nature et du ciel" (pp. 384–5).

This is clearly the Edenic "dumb-bell" shape, and our prose poem follows it. It ends with a full suggestion of the final apotheosis.

7 "Mallarmé's La Gloire," in *Writing in a Modern Temper*, edited by Mary Ann Caws, Saratoga, California: University of California Press (1984), pp. 136–45. I disagree with him in one small respect: the "cimes tard évanouies" refer probably to tree tops (so tall they catch the sun till late) associated with Fontainebleau, not mountain peaks. Generally he is solid and sensitive and brings out some subtle linguistic effects.

8 These parallel cycles, adding one of whole ages as in Hesiod, are treated in my *Coup de Dés* study, pp. 55 ff.

9 Compare the "nuit absconse" of church mysteries released from the folds of the priestly robe (analogous to folds in the mind, or of writing) by the violent thuds and flapping of the cloth in the springtime frenzy of *L'Ecclésiastique*. The *ombre* is thus probably ambiguous: it could be the sacred mysteries of the forest, the doubt and fear in his mind about the tourists who will spoil it.

10 I am thinking, of course, as Mallarmé would, of "All is but toys," "We are such stuff as dreams are made on," "A tale told by an idiot" and the like. This is typical of a Baroque mood, we know. The "Rien qui est la vérité" is the famous remark in his letter to Cazalis of March 1866. Note

that it is followed by a *gloire*: "glorieux mensonges," corresponding to the "quiétude menteuse."

11 The "automne sous les cieux" opens up to eternity, as does the "soucieux" which suggestively echoes it, as I noted in my study of the *Coup de Dés* in connection with that word (p. 295).

12 This single term stands out as did the initial "La Gloire," but as its opposite, as Lawler notes persuasively.

13 But the faun used the tree as a real phenomenon pitted against the maybe-illusory nymphs. That just shows the fluidity of his vision which saw all these reversibilities, eventually, "touched all the bases" sooner or later.

14 *Hommage à Richard Wagner.*

15 *Le Pitre châtié.*

13 Conflit

1 *Confrontation* is the title of a piece which covers much the same ground and could have figured in the collection, except for the fact that it would have seemed supererogatory.

2 In *L'Ecrivain et ses travaux* (Paris: Corti, 1967).

3 (Paris: Editions du Seuil, 1958).

4 *Letters au Castor* (Paris: Gallimard, 1984).

5 "Sur Tolstoï" (p. 873).

6 The "bohémiens" of *Le Grand Meaulnes* struck awe in the villagers; gypsies have long enjoyed this prestige, for example in D. H. Lawrence (*The Virgin and the Gypsy*).

7 See *L'Œuvre de Mallarmé*, especially the chapters devoted to pages 4 and 5.

8 *Le Livre de Mallarmé*, edited by Jacques Schérer (Paris: Gallimard, 1957), pp. 24ff.

9 In *La Nef*, 51 (1949), 38–49: Théodore Nathanson, "A Valvins, auprès de Mallarmé," p. 46.

10 Compare Sartre's existential psychology, which relates sexuality to physical preconditions, e.g. the famous passage of *L'Etre et le Néant* on the hole.

11 Compare "où qu'ils expirent en le charme et leur désuétude ... les bibelots abolis, sans usage" (p. 499), plus *Ses purs ongles*.

12 In *Aumône* the poet advises the tramp not to buy mundane bread with his alms, but to get drunk and rampage.

13 In the *Coup de Dés*, the *creux* of a wave is the womb of a future (crest) entity emerging from it in time; Valéry's *citerne* is a similar image in the *Cimetière marin*.

14 On page 8 of the *Coup de Dés* this *debout* stands for mankind's total rise, with a fatal hint in the undertone of *de boue*, corresponding to the earth mother here, who has contrary aims, as he puts it realistically in "Catholicisme" (*cf. Les Fleurs*).

15 "Selon un baptême ... Penche un salut."

16 "A propos du *Coup de dés*," in *Critique*, 416 (1982), 92–3.